"Michele Howe's newest book
another excellent addition to h
books. Don't take my word for it.
I guarantee you won't put it down any time soon. Then buy a couple of books for your close friends and family who may need inspiration in life."

—Rick Johnson, best-selling author of *How to Speak so Your Husband Will Listen* and *When Grandparents Become Parents*

"Grace and gratitude are two very powerful strategies in living a peaceful and victorious life. Michele has done a phenomenal job in providing practical examples, prayers, prompts, and specific action steps to help you develop habits of grace and gratitude. This book holds the power of testimonies and truth to help you unlock a deeper relationship with both Christ and others."

—Keri Kitchen, MEd, LPCC, NCC
Faith and Focus Coach and
Host of *The Every Day Royalty Podcast*

"Life can be so painful and disappointing and discouraging. How do we turn pain into dancing, sorrow into joy, and hopelessness into victory? *Grace & Gratitude for Everyday Life* will show you how to do just that. Through everyday life challenges, Michele guides you to love God more deeply, offer him your hurt, accept complete grace, and walk in gratitude."

—Lucille Williams, Author of *From Me to We*, *The Intimacy You Crave*, and *The Impossible Kid*

"Gratitude empowers us to be less judgmental, more tolerant, and graciously forgiving in the midst of rugged circumstances and heart hurts. In *Grace & Gratitude for Everyday Life*, author Michele Howe refocuses challenges through the lens of eternity where we find help, hope, and the reason we can live joyfully."

—PeggySue Wells, best-selling author of 30 books, including *The Ten Best Decisions a Single Mom Can Make*, *Homeless for the Holidays*, and *The Patent*

"In a world of contagious negativity, *Grace & Gratitude for Everyday Life* is a timely and gracious heart-check. Michele's gift of storytelling combined with her godly wisdom serves as a comprehensive guide to managing our attitudes and guarding against those things that would diminish the light we are called to be as believers. You hold in your hands a book packed with practical strategies to make gratitude your default response. When you turn the last page, you will understand that grace and gratitude are not only antidotes to negative emotions but weapons to wield that bring joy and contentment regardless of circumstances."

—Kathy Schwanke, speaker, Bible study author, mentor

"Author Michele Howe had me at 'grace.' *Grace & Gratitude for Everyday Life* gives this grin gal plenty to smile about. Like many of you, I've been going through some difficult circumstances. Trials that make me feel all alone. This book reminds me where to hang my hope, as I look to God for my contentment and joy. What do grace and gratitude have to do with everyday life? Everything! Or at least, they help make our experiences and perspective better along the way. Thanks to Michele for yet another helpful guide to finding abundant life as we change our focus from self to the Savior."

—Kathy Carlton Willis, God's Grin Gal, speaker
Author of *The Grin Gal's Guide to Joy*

"We all face disappointments and struggles. For our tough moments, *Grace & Gratitude for Everyday Life* offers the way to peace. Michele Howe brings uplifting insights through authentic personal stories and scripture. I recommend her inspiring recipe for contentment to all who hunger for hope."

—Tina Yeager, life coach, therapist, award-winning author, and host of the *Flourish-Meant Podcast*

GRACE & GRATITUDE FOR EVERYDAY LIFE

GRACE & GRATITUDE FOR EVERYDAY LIFE

MICHELE HOWE

an imprint of Hendrickson Publishing Group

Grace & Gratitude for Everyday Life

Published by Hendrickson Publishers
an imprint of Hendrickson Publishing Group
Hendrickson Publishers, LLC
P. O. Box 3473
Peabody, Massachusetts 01961-3473
www.hendricksonpublishinggroup.com

ISBN 978-1-4964-7163-5

Photo by Visual Stories || Micheile on Unsplash

Printed in the United States of America

First Printing — July 2022

Library of Congress Control Number: 2022933308

To Beau Hudson Ross

A blessed gift and a joy to behold.
Welcome to the world.
May your life shine brightly for Jesus!

Contents

Acknowledgments

I've said it before, and it bears repeating: Every book you hold in your hands is the product of the combined efforts and talents of many gifted individuals. While an author's name alone is featured on the front cover of a book, what you don't see are the names of the highly skilled people who work tirelessly behind the scenes. As the author of twenty-plus books, I've always been in awe of those who labor on behalf of myself and my work. I am both grateful and humbled by these individuals and their excellent work every single time I first hold a new book in my hands.

Let me share some names so that you, dear reader, can join me in saying thank you to these marvelously talented and God-honoring individuals whom I am so thankful to call my friends from afar. First, thank you, Patricia Anders; as editorial director at Hendrickson Publishers, you hold many responsibilities, and I cannot imagine the heavy workload you carry every day—seemingly with perfect ease. I am so thankful for you and for the friendship we now enjoy, and I'm so excited we can say together, "We did it. Again! Let's rejoice and give thanks!" Thanks also to assistant editor Sarah Welch and editorial assistant Kate Walker for your thoughtful and expert work on my book!

To Meg Rusick for marketing and promotion, Phil Frank for typesetting, Dave Pietrantonio for getting my book to the printer and out to the world, and to Sarah Slattery for her beautiful cover design, I thank you. Again. And again. And yet again. You are all much appreciated!

I also want to express my kindest appreciation to Bob Hostetler, who happily represents me at the Steve Laube Agency. I appreciate you and your diligent work on my behalf.

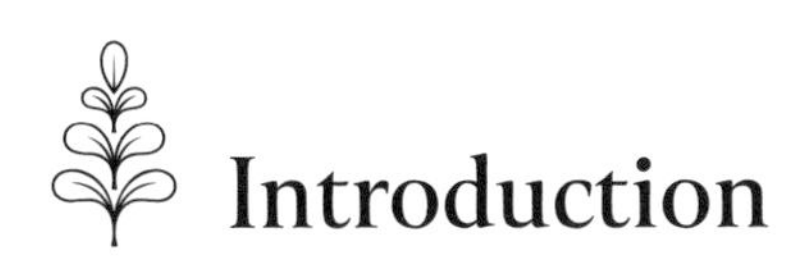

Introduction

A book is born in the mind of an author when they personally sense a felt need and then observe others struggling in similar fashion. This book, ***Grace & Gratitude for Everyday Life***, was first conceived in my heart and mind when I discovered the life-changing power of saying "thank you" to God no matter what the circumstance. This simple yet often difficult response is paramount in equipping us as Christ-followers to live as overcomers as we journey through life. I'm convinced of it. As we learn to make grace-filled gratitude our default response to every situation we face, we will discover that God's amazing peace envelops us from every side.

Instead of grumbling or grousing when we are disappointed or displeased, however, the apostle Paul encourages us to do as follows:

> Do everything without grumbling or arguing, so that you may become blameless and pure, children of God without fault in a warped and crooked generation. (Phil. 2:14)

> Do not be anxious about anything, but in every situation, by prayer and petition, with thanksgiving, present your requests to God. And the peace of God, which transcends all understanding, will guard your hearts and your minds in Christ Jesus. (Phil. 4:6–7)

Giving thanks, no matter what is happening all around us (or within us), isn't optional. It's simple obedience. And we know from countless passages throughout Scripture that God expects obedience from his children—not to harm us, but to make us both whole and holy.

On the worst of days, when we have a hard time finding something to be thankful about, it's always helpful to have some perspective. For example, do you have safe drinking water? More than one billion people in the world don't. Do you have enough food? More than 800 million don't. Do you have good eyesight, good hearing, decent clothes to wear, employment, family or friends who care about you, a safe place to live? The list goes on. If you think hard enough, you'll soon discover that you always have plenty of wonderful reasons to offer up thanks to your heavenly Father—your very breath of life is one of them! The problem is that most of us are in our own heads too much. We miss out on what's going on around us—especially in the beauty of nature, through a breathtaking sunset or the scent of a rose. All around us, God's grace showers us. And for this, we should indeed be grateful.

Throughout the pages of *Grace & Gratitude*, you'll discover how ordinary men and women have learned to give thanks in the face of suffering, trials, and faith-testing obstacles. You'll see that as they leaned in toward Jesus for the grace and strength to carry on, they were transformed by the power of the Holy Spirit. My prayer is that we all become humble students of God's word, and that we take him at his word and trust him hour by hour. He is indeed equally worthy of both our trust and our obedience—and, of course, our undying thanks!

Chapter 1

Why Grace & Gratitude?

Do everything without grumbling or arguing, so that you may become blameless and pure, children of God without fault in a warped and crooked generation. Then you will shine among them like stars in the sky as you hold firmly to the word of life.

Philippians 2:14–15

Gratitude never comes from avoiding difficulty but from finding yourself sustained through it. The degree of joy rises to the degree of gratitude, and the level of gratitude corresponds to the level of God's grace experienced in our suffering. God's sustaining providence brings relief, even when life becomes unspeakably difficult. Cultivating thankfulness today will allow us to cling to God's goodness and mercy in our darkest hours.

Randy Alcorn

Why grace? Why gratitude? Perhaps the better question is, why not grace and gratitude for everyday life? God, as our heavenly Father, knows us in intimate detail and carefully oversees every step (as well as every misstep) of our lives. So why does God place such importance on honing a consistently grace-filled, grateful heart? In short, because God knows how we thrive!

As we search through Scripture, we find a common theme presented throughout both the Old and New Testaments. That common cord began in the book of Genesis and was completed in the final words of the book of Revelation. It is clear that God commands his children to be thankful, and that a grateful heart is only possible when we are equipped by God's empowering grace. God repeatedly speaks through biblical characters in the Old Testament, instructing his beloved ones to be different and set apart from other nations in many ways—mostly by consistently adopting a humble, grateful attitude.

In the New Testament, Jesus and his apostles preach the same message: Be grateful. Live gratefully. Speak words of gratitude. As we study God's word, we read over and over again this same dynamic refrain, "Do everything without grumbling or arguing, so that you may become blameless and pure, children of God without fault in a warped and crooked generation" (Phil. 2:14). No matter what our difficulties might be, no matter how trying the circumstances are or how much suffering we're enduring, God's call for us is to respond gratefully, humbly, and with complete faith in his provision and outcome.

This is no small feat! However, when God issues a directive, he also provides the means to fulfill it. His promises to provide for our every need in each situation include every imaginable hardship we may be facing or may be called to face in the future. God calls Christians as his set-apart children who are to view all of life through the timeless, robust lens of eternity. As we choose to make gratitude our default response, God's supernatural grace, hope, and love swoop in to sustain us. Life is hard enough without falling into the self-sabotaging habit of grumbling and complaining, which then spins us into a downward spiral. God knows this, and if we're honest, deep down, we know it too. As we delve into the principle of honoring God by humbly trusting him, his light will begin to shine in our hearts and upon our difficulties. Because in God's economy, obedience is the supernatural key that unlocks the door to sustaining faith, hope, and love.

We can learn to become grateful despite any troubling circumstance, private pain, or personal disappointment. As we learn more about who God is and who he promises to be for us, we can respond with gratitude and humble, grace-filled trust. And we can be sure that our faith will grow stronger and more robust as we seek to obey God every day by intentionally choosing to say "thank you" no matter what the circumstances. "The more you suffer the greater your capacity to serve the Lord" (2 Cor. 4:17).

Learning to respond with a heart that beats with gratitude—even when we're facing what we might deem the worst scenario possible—allows us to receive God's supernatural grace, goodness, and constant provision. God wants us to be so sure of his faithfulness that whether we're facing good or bad circumstances, we can be confident of his sovereignty and his divine work to bring about both the good he wants for us and the glory that will be attributed to him in the process.

If you're still not convinced that a response of faith-bolstered, grace-filled gratitude is the best choice we can make, then keep on reading! God has great things in store for those who take him at his word, and he wants each of us to have the ability to live above and beyond our fickle emotions and ever-changing circumstances. This journey all begins and ends with a heart in tune with our heavenly Father's perfect love for us.

Take-away Action Thought

This week I will be mindful about the power of honing a grateful heart, even in the midst of challenging circumstances. I will determine to give thanks and cease grumbling, because I know that God is carefully overseeing every event in my life, whether large or small, and that I can trust him completely.

My Heart's Cry to You, O Lord

Father, I want to respond to every challenge, every difficulty, and every unwanted circumstance in humble trust, knowing that you are totally aware of what is happening in my life. Help me to choose grace-filled gratitude over grumbling as I exercise my faith muscles, knowing you intend only good for me. Equip me through the supernatural enabling of the Holy Spirit to obey your word and rest in complete assurance that you are always with me, sustaining me, strengthening me, and holding me close. Amen.

Practicing Grace & Gratitude

1. *Grace & gratitude from God.* "You will shine among them like stars in the sky as you hold firmly to the word of life." This week, I will direct my focus toward the heavens whenever I face something that challenges me to respond with obedient, faith-driven gratitude.

2. *Grace & gratitude in me.* "You may become blameless and pure, children of God without fault in a warped and crooked generation." Each evening, I will spend a few

minutes in prayer asking the Lord to help me to see my difficulties and challenges as tools to equip me to better serve him. I will spend time specifically giving thanks for God's perfect provision for me that day.

3. ***Grace & gratitude in life.*** "Do everything without grumbling or arguing." Each day, I will reflect on my attitude and be mindful about whether or not my first response to unexpected or unwanted circumstances was one of humble acceptance or sinful grumbling.

Chapter 2

A Grace-Filled Perspective Changes Everything

Honor one another above yourselves. Never be lacking in zeal, but keep your spiritual fervor, serving the Lord. Be joyful in hope, patient in affliction, faithful in prayer.

Romans 12:10–12

In the midst of chaos, the Spirit often gives us a simple and clear mission, such as choosing to trust in God's love, listening to another person, helping someone in his or her need, or preparing lunch. Your God has made you a partner in bringing his kingdom to earth. Look around to see what he is doing and how he might want you to participate with him.

Edward Welch

Emma was on hold for the third time that early fall morning as she waited for her mom's oncology nurse to answer her current list of questions. As she waited, she thought once more about how quickly their lives had changed. A single woman in her mid-thirties, Emma had become her terminally ill mother's full-time caregiver. Years earlier, she had lost her father when he was killed during a dangerous military operation. Since that tragedy, it had been just the two of them: Emma and her mom, Sara. And a mighty twosome they were.

Emma and Sara were always among the first to volunteer to care for those in need through their local church, in their neighborhood, and among their many beloved friends. While they didn't have any family to speak of except each other, they counted themselves rich beyond measure in their relationships with their community. This mother and daughter duo were well loved and celebrated for their generous, selfless lives.

When Sara began to recognize that something felt wrong physically, she went to her family physician who ordered all the appropriate tests. Within a week's time, she was given the life-shattering news that she had terminal cancer. Stunned, Sara's first thought was of Emma. How would her daughter cope with this news? How would she get through this ordeal? How could Sara tell her only child that she was about to become an orphan?

All these questions and many more flooded Sara's thoughts as she drove back home. As soon as Emma heard Sara's car pull into their driveway, she ran out to meet her mom. Emma broke down and cried when her mom told her the devastating news. Tears continued to spill as Emma and Sara sat side by side on the couch, talking and praying, and then talking and praying some more.

Finally, they realized they had to talk specifics. Difficult as it was, Sara and Emma started to form a practical plan for Sara's care. It wouldn't be easy. It wouldn't be without stress and heart-rending pain and sorrow, but both mother and daughter realized they had to choose an attitude of joy even now. Having survived the death of a spouse and father, respectively, they had been down this difficult road together before. And they had learned a lot as they had grieved and then slowly healed from their mutual loss.

So for the hours they were given today, both Emma and Sara chose to focus on God's past and present faithfulness to them. They chose to live in the grace that God supplied for this hour and this day alone, fully confident that he who promised to supply their every need was faithful. As they embraced an attitude of joy, that single grace-filled step of obedience enabled them to face the future with an eternal perspective that changed everything.

Given Emma and Sara's robust history of faith in God, they were more prepared than most to turn their fears and mourning into an opportunity to trust God moment by moment, day by day. When they turned to him swiftly and without hesitation, God showered them with an otherworldly sense of peace and calm. Still, given the suddenness of Sara's diagnosis, both Sara and Emma sometimes found themselves having to regroup emotionally by turning repeatedly to the Lord as they prayed through all their questions, doubts, and fears.

They felt all the accompanying intense emotions that everyone experiences when suddenly blindsided by terrible news. Emma and her mom cried out their sorrow until they had no more tears to shed. They felt the weight of what Sara might have to suffer physically before she died. And they each spent much time in solitude before God, asking him to give them grace for just today.

This very act of turning toward God rather than away from him in the midst of their trouble made all the difference. Even in their desperation, Emma and Sara knew that the only place where help was to be found was in the person and presence of God. They knew the only one who could supply them with the grace they needed to handle each day's challenges was God, and they believed that through the Holy Spirit's empowering strength, they would be able to endure this ordeal. Because they knew where and with whom they would find their help, Emma and Sara could rest in God's sovereignty and perfect plan for their lives. And they did.

This mother and daughter duo revealed to all who knew and loved them that when we know our Savior, we can also know peace in the midst of every storm. Emma and Sara learned to pray and give thanks at the end of every day. They learned to view their difficult circumstances through the lens of eternity, knowing full well that God was weaving a beautiful tapestry of faith that would become a legacy that would outlive them both. In truth, that was their prayer—that God would use this heartbreaking situation to shine the brilliance of Jesus' perfect love to all who knew them, and that this eternal, saving truth would transform hearts of unbelief to those of faith.

Take-away Action Thought

When I feel my emotions spiraling out of control, I will find a solitary place to be alone with the Lord and express my feelings to him. As I cry out my pain, I will remember to cry out to God for his comfort, peace, and sustaining grace.

My Heart's Cry to You, O Lord

Father, help me to put the full weight of my pain into your capable, loving hands. Help me to know your perfect peace in this heartbreaking situation. I know that you promise to give me all that I need to handle the storms of life, and right now this storm is raging around me. Give me your sustaining grace and strength to focus on the needs of my loved one. Remind me that you are the God of all comfort and that you are close by me day and night. Help me to remember that the suffering of this life will soon be over and that we will forever be in your heavenly kingdom where sorrow is no more. Amen.

Practicing Grace & Gratitude

1. *Grace & gratitude from God.* "Never be lacking in zeal, but keep your spiritual fervor, serving the Lord." As I face this heartbreaking situation, I will spend a few moments each evening writing down at least five blessings of the day. Then I'll spend time thanking the Lord for his mercies, which are new every morning.
2. *Grace & gratitude in me.* "Be joyful in hope, patient in affliction, faithful in prayer." This week, I will focus on maintaining a joyful attitude. Despite any setbacks or disappointments, I will pray daily for God's grace to enable me to not complain but rather to give thanks in every situation.
3. *Grace & gratitude in life.* "Honor one another above yourselves." Before getting up each morning this week, I will spend a few minutes praying for those I know are in need. I'll pray specifically for their unique circumstance and plan simple ways to ease their burdens.

Chapter 3

A Right View of God Makes Us Grateful

I will make an everlasting covenant with them: I will never stop doing good to them, and I will inspire them to fear me, so that they will never turn away from me. I will rejoice in doing them good and will assuredly plant them in this land with all my heart and soul.

Jeremiah 32:40–41

What I had to do was to decide if I would trust Him, even when my heart ached. We must learn to obey God one choice at a time; we must also learn to trust God one circumstance at a time. Trusting God is not a matter of my feelings but of my will. I never feel like trusting God when adversity strikes, but I can choose to do so even when I don't feel like it. That act of the will, though, must be based on belief, and belief must be based on truth.

Jerry Bridges

Victoria completed her online order and sat back smiling. She had just sent a batch of inspirational greeting cards to folks in her church family who were sick and convalescing at home. As a senior citizen herself, Victoria empathized with her fellow elders who were facing increasingly difficult health challenges as they aged. Victoria had never forgotten the moment she herself found out she had Multiple Sclerosis. Even though many years had passed since then, that difficult life season was forever seared into her memory.

Yes, she prayed silently, *it really has been fifteen years since my diagnosis, and what a long, hard year that was. I remember, Lord, how devastated I was when my physician gently shared the news. I can recall everything about that day—her office, the wall décor, the stained-oak furniture, and even her family photos that faced me as I tried to deal with that frightening news. And then, how I fought against accepting that I actually had MS. I just couldn't and wouldn't believe it!*

Victoria closed her eyes and reminisced about how she had to first accept the scary diagnosis, and then accept the truth that God had allowed it and she needed to trust him through it all. Oh, how hard it was for her to believe that he could take something so terrible as MS and use it to help her see him more clearly. *But you did use it, and as horrible as that season was battling against MS, you kept me close to you and you sustained me every minute of every day.*

Smiling now, Victoria opened her eyes and began to list the folks from her church who needed some encouragement and a reminder of how faithful and loving God is, especially when we need him most.

Isn't it a wonderful truth that God never leaves us to fight life's battles on our own? He promises to never stop doing good to us, he inspires us to be in awe of him, and he rejoices in taking even the worst that happens in this life and transforming it. Yes, God promises good to us even when our circumstances and our emotions scream the opposite. And yes, sometimes it is difficult to see past our present suffering and view our trials through an eternal lens. But we must learn to trust him, as Jerry Bridges notes: "Trusting God is not a matter of my feelings but of my will. I never feel like trusting God when adversity strikes, but I can choose to do so even when I don't feel like it."

When we choose to fully trust God despite our pain and suffering, we can begin to reap the benefits of that obedience. God strengthens our faith, enlarges our vision, and pours out his grace on us to respond in faith and have in confidence in God's ability to supply our every need. As Victoria discovered during her battle with MS, every time she started to grow fearful but then stopped herself short by reciting Bible verses out loud, God became bigger and her fears, worries, and anxieties became smaller. She recognized it was a moment-by-moment decision—either to give way to her fear and trembling, or to choose to trust God even when she was unsure of the outcome. That life-defining choice is exactly what she encourages other hurting individuals to do as well.

Take-away Action Thought

When I feel afraid, I will exercise my will and trust in God. I will go directly to Scripture and recite his promises of perfect provision out loud. Then I'll give thanks for the grace and strength I'm confident God will send, moment by moment.

My Heart's Cry to You, O Lord

Father, today I received some of the most frightening news I could imagine. I want to honor you by trusting you to supply all my needs, but I'm afraid. Help me to believe your promises to stay close to me during my suffering and to bless me with the strength, grace, and peace I need. I know how weak I am, Lord, and so I rely on your supernatural strength to help me trust you from one moment to the next. Help me to remember your life-giving promises. Strengthen my faith during this trial. I want to emerge from it knowing you more intimately and with the confidence to share this love with others. Amen.

Practicing Grace & Gratitude

1. *Grace & gratitude from God.* "I will make an everlasting covenant with them: I will never stop doing good to them." This week, I'll spend time each day journaling about God's past faithfulness to me, focusing on those specific moments when he transformed hardship into something beautiful and good.

2. *Grace & gratitude in me.* "I will inspire them to fear me, so that they will never turn away from me." Each day, I will locate verses that have the word *fear* in them and explore more fully how fearing God is a good thing, because we learn how glorious he is and how we should be in awe of him.

3. *Grace & gratitude in life.* "I will rejoice in doing them good and will assuredly plant them in this land with all my heart and soul." At least two times this week, I will send out cards of encouragement to those I know dealing with debilitating circumstances. I will share with

them how God faithfully met me in my time of need and brought blessing and goodness to me, despite the challenges I was facing.

Chapter 4

The Link between Grace & Gratitude

I love the LORD, for he heard my voice;
he heard my cry for mercy.
Because he turned his ear to me,
I will call on him as long as I live. . . .
The LORD is gracious and righteous;
our God is full of compassion.
The LORD protects the unwary;
when I was brought low, he saved me.
Return to your rest, my soul,
for the LORD has been good to you.

Psalm 116:1–2, 5–7

When I get up in the morning, I do try to make it a practice to do some of my praying first thing in the morning. It's a good thing to talk to God before you start talking to anybody else.

Elisabeth Elliot

As Melissa and her husband, Jake, drove to church, they discussed dinner plans for later that day. They looked forward to spending that time with their two sons and their families. What a joy it was for Melissa to have both her sons living in the same city again, along with daughters-in-law and grandchildren too. Her mother's heart rejoiced at the thought. As Jake drove up to the four-way stop sign right before the driveway for their church, Melissa noticed a familiar car across the road.

"Oh look, it's Josh! He's waving at us," Melissa said to Jake.

"And look over there!" Jake said as he proceeded through the four-way stop. "There's Jeremy!"

When Melissa glanced to where Jake pointed, she saw their other son at the stop sign waiting to cross the intersection as well. Melissa smiled again and now waved at Jeremy. Shaking her head in amazement, she said, "Look what God just did. He brought our entire family to the same intersection at the very same time. Isn't that something?"

"Yes it is," Jake responded with a big smile.

"And in more ways than one," she said returning his smile. She then thought to herself that God had indeed brought them all together at this exact moment in time both in life and in faith.

As Jake drove into the parking lot and searched for a space, Melissa remembered the not-so-happy times in the not-so-distant past, when neither of their sons' lives were God-honoring. In high school, both Josh and Jeremy had professed faith in Christ and lived out what looked like genuine saving faith. But once they left home for college, they seemed to turn away from following Christ. Four long years of watching their two sons live in wild rebellion almost broke Melissa's and Jake's hearts. But they never stopped praying for their sons. They asked God to draw them back to himself, and that he would create a thirst within the boys' hearts that would not be quenched.

During those days, Melissa dropped to her knees beside her bed every morning to intercede on their behalf. Before she talked to anyone else—even Jake!—Melissa poured her heart out to God, pleading with him to bring her sons back to their faith. Remembering those pain-wracked early morning vigils, Melissa felt a sudden rush of gratitude for what God had done to bring them now to this point—meeting at church to worship together again! She thanked God again for his faithfulness and the sustaining grace he provided that enabled her to not give up on them during those difficult years of rebellion.

Most of us have heard the age-old question: "What came first, the chicken or the egg?" That same parallel principle might well be asked here. What comes first? Grace or gratitude? Because you can't have one without the other. If you're a Christian, you have been given the grace of God through the supernatural work of the Holy Spirit. You have also been commanded by God to hone a heart of gratitude. And if your heart is in a position of obedience, then your mouth can speak out that grace-filled gratitude no matter what circumstances you're facing.

One of the challenges for Melissa and Jake was how they chose to talk about their sons while Josh and Jeremy lived in rebellion. When the sons made choices that willfully defied God's pattern for living, their parents struggled to keep conversations from spiraling into negativity and despair. Over and over, Melissa and Jake rehashed the escalating foolishness of their sons' choices, and their mutual verbal hand-wringing only made them feel worse.

Finally, Jake talked with Melissa about their debilitating conversational habits, and they decided to change how they spoke about Josh and Jeremy. Melissa found that it helped her immensely to get up early, drop to her knees, and pray before she did anything else. Jake discovered it worked best for him to use his commute to work to listen to his audio Bible and then pray before he left the car to go into his office.

Both Melissa and Jake asked God daily for grace to handle that difficult season with their sons. They also made sure they spent generous amounts of intentional energy thanking God for his many blessings, despite the pain the boys caused them.

This wise couple recounts these two key heart attitudes as the one-two spiritual punch that enabled them to continue praying and living with a robust hope. Early on in the battle, Melissa and Jake learned that the important life lessons they talked about with others would powerfully affect how they handled their difficult circumstances. They needed to remember to always respond with a refreshing, hope-filled heart of gratitude that is contagious to a watching world.

Take-away Action Thought

When difficulties overwhelm me and I begin to fall into emotional despair, I will remember to give thanks for God's intimate knowledge of the situation and for his sovereign rule over all creation. My heart will be steadfast because of God's great compassion for me, and I will proclaim aloud verses that proclaim God's perfect provision.

My Heart's Cry to You, O Lord

Father, this current situation is breaking my heart. Day by day, I cry out to you for help, and I am so thankful that I know that you are attentive to my every prayer. Please help me to remember that the words I speak to others make a powerful difference in my heart attitude. Help me to not spiral into emotional despair but instead to speak forth words of hope-filled promise because I know you are in control. Give me your grace to say my thanks, even when the night is darkest. I trust in you as my redeemer and my deliverer. Amen.

Practicing Grace & Gratitude

1. ***Grace & gratitude from God.*** "The Lord protects the unwary; when I was brought low, he saved me." With Bible and journal in hand, I'll look up specific verses in the Psalms that tell of God's grace and strength. I'll then write these in my journal to review each day.
2. ***Grace & gratitude in me.*** "Because he turned his ear to me, I will call on him as long as I live." This week, I'll commit to listening to the book of Psalms on audio when I'm walking, in the car, or working around my home. At the end of each day, I'll read these same psalms before bedtime and thank God for how attentive he is toward me.
3. ***Grace & gratitude in life.*** "The Lord is gracious and righteous; our God is full of compassion." Every day this week, I'll write down daily specific instances (both large and small) of God's gracious compassion toward me. Despite the struggles I'm facing, I will choose to focus on honing a grace-filled, grateful heart attitude.

Chapter 5

Growing a Grateful Heart One Thought at a Time

When hard pressed, I cried to the Lord;
he brought me into a spacious place.
The Lord is with me; I will not be afraid.
What can mere mortals do to me?

Psalm 118:5–6

If we go on without gratitude—choosing to be bitter, constantly bemoaning our fate—we force ourselves to live in already unhappy conditions with the added drag of our gloomy disposition. Unwilling to stay mindful of the blessings we enjoy in spite of our difficulties, as well as the strength and sensitivity God grows best in us through hardship and loss, we sacrifice peace. We sacrifice contentment. We sacrifice relationships—freedom and grace and joy.

Nancy Leigh DeMoss

"You're the most negative person I've ever met!" Luke told his teenage sister Liesel. "Why can't you ever focus just once on the positive? You know, this move isn't easy for me either." With this parting reminder, Luke stormed out of the room. Liesel wanted to yell back at her older brother, but she didn't. She knew he was right. When life didn't go according to her plan, watch out world! She had tried half-heartedly to be cheerful and upbeat, but there was something inside of her that continually dragged her into a negative, complaining space.

Liesel stood in the hallway for a few moments before going into her room and shutting the door. *Who wouldn't be upset about moving twice in one year? I've just gotten to know people. I finally have some friends!* she fumed to herself. *Now, just because of Dad's job, we have to move right after Christmas. Why don't they think about me and how I'm affected by it!* She proceeded to talk herself into a frenzy of angry, bitter resentment, which made her feel even worse than before Luke had chastised her for complaining. Liesel hung her head and started to cry as she started to think about what Luke said.

This is Luke's last year of high school before he leaves for college, and I'm sure he doesn't want to move either. He's hurting too. But how does Luke handle these moves so much better than me? He never complains or gets angry about it, he just . . . accepts it. Even though we're in the same family, we're so different. I wish I could be more like him. But I'm not. I get angry. Where Luke sees the good in something, I get mad and complain. Luke always manages to make the best of it.

Liesel felt ashamed of her selfish reaction. Once again, she had been focusing only on herself and her own feelings. She forgot there were three other people in her family feeling the same loss and disappointment. *I want to change, Lord,* she prayed. *Please help me. Forgive me for thinking only about myself. You've been so good to me. Starting right now, I want to be more like Luke and think about what's good in a situation instead of what's bad. Help me to be grateful instead of always complaining!*

Taking our thoughts captive, one at a time, is the only way we can learn to overcome our natural tendency to complain and get upset about the difficulties that invade our lives. As Liesel discovered when her brother rebuked her for her consistently sinful responses to challenges, we alone are responsible for how we view the obstacles that God has allowed to enter our lives.

We may be tempted to complain and get angry at others' decisions that impact us in ways we don't like. We may even be tempted to complain and get angry at God, because after all, he is sovereign. But all the complaining in the world won't alter or remove the difficulties we must face. As Nancy Leigh DeMoss so wisely states, "Unwilling to stay mindful of the blessings we enjoy in spite of our difficulties, as well as the strength and sensitivity God grows best in us through hardship and loss, we sacrifice peace."

When God places us into challenging, painful situations for reasons only he knows, our first and best response is to humbly bow our heads and give thanks that he knows best. We can be sure because the Bible tells us so: that his love for us is greater than our limited understanding. We know because of Jesus' sacrifice on the cross that his care is superior to any human love or comfort of our own making.

One thought at a time. It's up to us to make our thoughts count for eternity and not waste them by petty complaints about God's perfect plan for our lives. Through the grace of God, we can learn to make gratitude our default response to any challenge we face.

Take-away Action Thought

When I am tempted to complain, I will stop myself by the grace of God from going down any path that leads to anger, disappointment, or bitterness. Instead, I will thank God for every blessing I can think of, from the smallest to the greatest. I will learn to make this attitude of gratitude my default response to any challenges that come my way.

My Heart's Cry to You, O Lord

Father, I was tempted again today to let loose a litany of complaints about everything that's going wrong right now. I want to learn to respond with a heart full of gratitude and thanks, no matter how challenging my life may be. But honestly, I'm not there yet. Please help me to have self-control through the Holy Spirit to silence my complaints, and give you thanks through the grace you supply. Although I may not like what you're allowing into my life right now, I know your perfect love for me exceeds my imperfect understanding. Thank you for being patient with me as I learn how to break my complaining habit once and for all. Amen.

Practicing Grace & Gratitude

1. *Grace & gratitude from God.* "When hard pressed, I cried to the Lord." Each day this week, I'll write ten specific blessings from the Lord in my journal. Once I've written down these blessings, I'll fill in the specifics about how God has blessed my life with each of them. I'll also include the details of how God worked on my behalf for my good.

2. *Grace & gratitude in me.* "The Lord is with me; I will not be afraid." Instead of dwelling on the negative or difficult challenges before me, I'll make an attitude of gratitude my default response. I will purposefully speak my thanks out loud to God first thing in the morning and before I go to sleep.
3. *Grace & gratitude in life.* "He brought me into a spacious place." When life looks scary because of the unknowns, I'll spend time in the book of Psalms. I will write down specific verses that encourage me to put the full weight of my trust in God, who is in control of my past, my present, and my future.

Chapter 6

A Grateful Heart Outshines Our Circumstances

Above all, love each other deeply, because love covers over a multitude of sins. Offer hospitality to one another without grumbling. Each of you should use whatever gift you have received to serve others, as faithful stewards of God's grace in its various forms.

1 Peter 4:8–10

If God has given us a gift, it's never only for ourselves. It's always to be offered back to Him and very often it has repercussions for the life of the world. Jesus offered Himself to be bread for the life of the world. He said the bread that I will give is my body and I give it for the life of the world. For a Christian, the pattern is Jesus. What did He do? He offered Himself, a perfect and complete sacrifice, for the love of God. And you and I should be prepared, also, to be broken bread and poured out wine for the life of the world.

Elisabeth Elliot

As Megan listened intently to her daughter Emily excitedly tell her about her mother-in-law's wonderful recent visit to their home, she felt small inside. *What's the matter with me?* Megan asked herself after she hung up the phone. *I love Emily's mother-in-law, Linda. Although we might not see each other often, I actually consider her a friend. So why am I so upset when I hear about the wonderful ways that she blesses my daughter and her family? Am I simply jealous that Linda has so much more disposable income than we do?* As Megan walked into her laundry room to toss in another load of dirty clothes, her mind lingered on what Emily had just told her about Linda's nice visit. *Lord, why can't I spoil my grandchildren the same way Linda does? Why can't we treat our kids and our grandkids to meals out whenever we visit them? You know my mother's heart wants to give to them the same way Linda does.* Megan wanted to cry.

From her perspective, it had always been this way. She knew how to budget since she and her husband, Dan, had been a single-income family. They decided even before children came along that they wanted Megan at home full time raising their children. And while Megan never once regretted that decision, it was admittedly hard sometimes. Like right now, for instance—when her heart longed to splurge on her grandchildren, the family budget said no. In the past, she had learned to be creative with her gift-giving, so she wasn't a stranger to shopping for good deals, making homemade gifts, and setting aside as much as she could throughout the year for birthdays and seasonal holiday giving. Still, this morning's conversation stung.

Lord, Megan prayed, *this is a heart issue, not a money issue, and we both know it. How many times have I silently complained about not having enough money? Far too often, I admit. Please help me to see the bigger picture here. I may not have the financial resources to give lavishly, but I can love lav-*

ishly and shower that love on my family. I can pray for each of my beloved grandchildren. I can write them endearing, funny letters. I can teach them how to garden and cook and be creative themselves. But above all, I can tell them about Jesus. Thank you for reminding me that you have gifted me in many ways to love my children and grandchildren that will impact them for all eternity. Amen.

Whether we are gifted with material means or personal talents and abilities, God expects us to give from our hearts. He wants us to recognize and rejoice in the truth that he, as the giver of all good gifts, has an eternal plan specifically tailored for each of us. Our lives are under the careful control of our sovereign heavenly Father who works all things together for our good and his glory. Whether we have a little or a lot is in God's hands.

But in the real world, this spiritual dynamic can be hard to accept. As fragile humans living with the stain of sin within our hearts, we admittedly do struggle with wanting "more" sometimes. Thus, Megan's longing to give "more" to her family is understandable. But perhaps God wanted to do a deeper work in Megan's heart by teaching her that wanting "more" is a contentment issue. When we focus on what we do not have (or cannot give), we forfeit a happy, grateful heart that rises above our circumstances.

As Megan realized, when we covet something God has decided to withhold from us, material or otherwise, we must confess our lack of contentment as sin and instead begin thanking the Lord for his abundant blessings. Megan understood that the bigger picture wasn't about giving material goods to those she loved. It was prayerfully coming before God and asking him to show her how to give what matters most and lasts for all eternity. Sure, it's wonderful to be able to give materially to those we love. But at the end of our lives, the love we gave away in the hope of bringing others to a saving faith in Jesus is the only gift that matters. Give the gift that will stand the test of all eternity: tell your loved ones about Jesus and live your life to reflect Jesus in every situation.

Take-away Action Thought

When I find myself giving way to discontentment about what God has supplied for me, I will confess this lack of gratitude as sin and begin giving thanks for his many blessings and perfect provision. I will not allow envy or jealousy to take root in my heart.

My Heart's Cry to You, O Lord

Father, I struggled again today with a longing to have more so that I could give more. Please help me to hone a heart of grace-filled gratitude instead of desiring what you have chosen not to give me. You have always met my needs; in fact, you have frequently blessed me far beyond my means. I thank you for that. But I still admit that I sometimes find myself wanting "more." Please help me to make the best use of the gifts you have given me and to always remember that I can give lavishly of love, prayer, and service—and that those gifts can make an eternal impact. Amen.

Practicing Grace & Gratitude

1. *Grace & gratitude from God.* "Each of you should use whatever gift you have received to serve others." This week, I will write down whatever God has given me by way of material gifts as well as talents and abilities that I can use to bless others. Once I have my list, I will prayerfully write down one person's name next to each gift and make a practical plan to bless that person.

2. *Grace & gratitude in me.* "Above all, love each other deeply, because love covers over a multitude of sins." Each evening this week, I'll spend time in prayer asking the Lord to reveal to me if I'm envying anyone because of what God has blessed them with. If I'm holding resentment or bitterness against anyone, I'll confess that sin to God and begin praying for that person as a way to counter my own wayward heart.

3. *Grace & gratitude in life.* "Offer hospitality to one another without grumbling." Using my gift list from above, I'll start planning practical ways to show love and service to my family and friends. If I'm using lack of monetary resources as an excuse not to be hospitable, I'll get creative in finding ways to invite others into my home without spending a lot of money.

Chapter 7

God Blesses Us as We Gratefully Forgive

Cleanse me with hyssop, and I will be clean;
  wash me, and I will be whiter than snow.
Let me hear joy and gladness;
  let the bones you have crushed rejoice.
Hide your face from my sins
  and blot out all my iniquity.
Create in me a pure heart, O God,
  and renew a steadfast spirit within me.
Do not cast me from your presence
  or take your Holy Spirit from me.
Restore to me the joy of your salvation
  and grant me a willing spirit, to sustain me.

Psalm 51:7–12

You may be trying to hide past sins that you still regret. For them, you need a forgiveness story from Scripture that can become your story. When you are forgiven much, you love Jesus and others much. You are thankful, rather than guilty.

Edward Welch

Rachel sat nervously twisting her hands as she waited for the nurse to call her name. She had waited years for this appointment with her obstetrician. But now that it was happening, she was terrified that her doctor might discover some unforeseen complications, given her medical history. According to Rachel's calculations, she was twelve weeks pregnant. She sure felt pregnant—sick in the morning, exhausted all day long, and battling up and down emotions as well. She had never carried a baby this long before, and so she was justifiably concerned.

That single thought made tears spring to her eyes. While she tried to covertly wipe away the wetness on her cheeks, she couldn't escape the feeling that she didn't deserve this blessed baby. Rachel was happily married to Scott, whom she met at the Christian college they both attended. They had gotten married the month after they both graduated, and three years later, they were expecting their first child. Scott was jubilant about becoming a father. Rachel vacillated between being immensely grateful and feeling shame-ridden. She struggled to believe that God had really blessed her with a baby after her past choices.

Aside from Rachel's immediate family and Scott, only a few people knew that Rachel had aborted two babies in high school. At the time, she had been dating a young man she met at the fast-food restaurant where they both worked. Unbeknown to her parents, Rachel had two abortions in two years.

The trauma she experienced in the months that followed left her spiraling out of control emotionally. At the lowest point of her young life, Rachel finally confessed her painful secret to her parents. They worked together as a family to help Rachel heal, and soon after, she became a Christian. Rachel's parents helped her find a biblical counselor who spent generous amounts of time talking her through her struggles and helping her to forgive herself so that she could live free in Christ.

Fast-forwarding to the present day, Rachel still struggles with her past decisions, still struggling to forgive herself and truly believe that God has cleansed her and forgiven her. Sitting in the doctor's office surrounded by pregnant women and their little ones, she had to keep reminding herself that all was forgiven in Jesus. She was a new creation. The old was gone and the new had just begun! With quiet deliberation, Rachel pulled out her phone and scrolled through her favorite Bible verses. As she read each one over and over, her emotions calmed, and she began to thank the Lord for the blessing this new life would be to her and Scott.

Hearing Rachel's story makes me consider the sins in my own life both before and after I became a Christian. If I spend too much time mentally revisiting them, feelings of remorse and regret can paralyze me both emotionally and spiritually. But, as Rachel discovered, once we have asked for forgiveness for our sins, God forgives them—and he chooses to forget them. We are no longer considered guilty for our sins. Praise the Lord!

Yet still, many of us are tempted to linger in those memories of our past sinful choices. We remember the people we hurt. We remember the innocents who were injured. We remember every single detail and accompanying emotion. It can become easy for us to grow spiritually despondent, which holds us back from living the life God has blessed us with today.

In no way do I dismiss or minimize the emotional, mental, and spiritual battle that takes place when we, as forgiven people of God, choose to take him at his word and accept his forgiveness. As humans with limited understanding, we may mistakenly believe we have to continue to "pay" for our sins, but the Bible is clear: "If we confess our sins, he is faithful and just and will forgive us our sins and purify us from all unrighteousness" (1 John 1:9). Even more powerful is the fact that God forgave King David for his adultery with Bathsheba and subsequent murder of her husband. Psalm 51 stands as a beacon of hope for all who feel they have sinned too grievously for God's cleansing and healing love.

Our choice, like Rachel's, is to stand firm on this precious promise of forgiveness no matter how much our vacillating emotions might tempt us from one moment to the next. *We are forgiven!* We must then live out this gift so that we can exist in the present, free of past regrets that paralyze us from loving and serving as God would have us do.

Sometimes, we have to take ourselves by the hand and walk directly to the source of all our comfort and consolation. We go directly to God's word. We read it. We meditate on it. We memorize it. We give thanks for its life-giving, freeing truth of forgiveness and then, as often as necessary, we repeat these steps all to the glory of God.

Take-away Action Thought

When I get mired in regret because of my past sins, I will open God's word and start reading verses that declare the fullness of his forgiveness. I will write down several of these key verses and take them with me throughout the day to read and reread out loud.

My Heart's Cry to You, O Lord

Father, here I am again getting stuck in the past by foolishly revisiting my sins and mistakes. I'm feeling full of regret and sorrow. I know better than to linger in the past, thinking about how different my life might have been had I not chosen the path I did. But I can't go back and undo these choices. What I can do today, however, is walk in your forgiveness and freedom and be grateful that you are in the business of restoration and redemption. Thank you, Lord, for your unconditional love toward me and the forgiveness you offer fully and freely. Amen.

> Cleanse me with hyssop, and I will be clean;
> wash me, and I will be whiter than snow.
> Let me hear joy and gladness;
> let the bones you have crushed rejoice.
> Hide your face from my sins
> and blot out all my iniquity.
> Create in me a pure heart, O God,
> and renew a steadfast spirit within me.
> Do not cast me from your presence
> or take your Holy Spirit from me.
> Restore to me the joy of your salvation
> and grant me a willing spirit, to sustain me.

Practicing Grace & Gratitude

1. *Grace & gratitude from God.* "Cleanse me with hyssop, and I will be clean; wash me, and I will be whiter than snow." Before closing my eyes to sleep, I'll spend a few moments recounting my day and give thanks to God for his ever-present grace and blessings. I will also give thanks for his full and free forgiveness through Jesus.

2. *Grace & gratitude in me.* "Create in me a pure heart, O God, and renew a steadfast spirit within me." Each evening this week, I will spend time reading one proverb on wise living. As I read, I'll make notes of any verses that are particularly pertinent to my week and the activities and responsibilities God has given me.
3. *Grace & gratitude in life.* "Restore to me the joy of your salvation and grant me a willing spirit, to sustain me." Each day this week, I will recite this verse before I go to work or interact with others. I'll be mindful of the many times I've had to ask God for forgiveness and how he is always gracious to grant it. Likewise, I'll be prepared and ready to forgive when asked by others. I will always remember how God always restores the joy of his salvation to me and how he continuously sustains me.

Chapter 8

Our Eternal Perspective Overflows to Grace & Gratitude

For we do not have a high priest who is unable to empathize with our weaknesses, but we have one who has been tempted in every way, just as we are—yet he did not sin. Let us then approach God's throne of grace with confidence, so that we may receive mercy and find grace to help us in our time of need.

Hebrews 4:15–16

Failure and the fear of it are a perfect opportunity. A constant string of successes is a grave danger. We don't tend to grow in humility and humanity through our success. Failure can lead us to dependence and trust in our successful and competent God. That is true success.

Edward Welch

There he goes again, Henry groused silently. ***Always moaning and bellyaching about something.*** Henry set the dish he was washing back into the soapy water, dried his hands, and took a deep, determined breath before answering his father's impatient call. Henry stepped from the tiny kitchen into the hall. With each step, his dad's irritated voice boomed louder. Grinding his teeth until his jaw ached, Henry said a quick prayer for grace to handle whatever had upset his father this time.

"The television isn't working right. I can't watch the game if I can't see it! Fix it, will you?" Alan demanded, throwing the television remote control at Henry. Lunging to catch the remote before it dropped on the hardwood floor and the batteries spilled out, Henry took a deep breath before responding. "Dad, you don't have to be so impatient. I'll try to move the antenna around so you can get a clearer picture, but these old wire antennas don't always do the job. Throwing the remote at me won't help you see anything better."

Henry saw his dad's face getting redder and redder. ***Here it comes***, he thought, steeling himself for the angry retort he knew was imminent. "You know I'm not made of money!" Alan yelled. "I can't afford that expensive cable package you're always nagging me about. Stop telling me how to live my life. I know what I want and how I want it done. Now just fix it and leave me alone!"

Leave you alone? Henry thought. ***On days like this, I wish I could.***

He fiddled with the antenna until the television screen became clearer. "Dad, it's as clear as I can get it." Grunting his response, Alan fixed his eyes on the screen and completely ignored his son. Henry shook his head in irritation. ***Just once, I'd like to hear my father ask politely and then say thank you!*** Back in the kitchen again, he finished doing the dishes his father had used earlier in the day. As he washed, rinsed, and dried,

Henry began to feel a sickening remorse fill his heart. ***I feel like a terrible son, Lord. I get so angry—I'm going to lose it one of these days. Here I am a Christian and my elderly father is not, and I'm feeling anything but love for him. Please help me to keep my cool and be patient and kind. Every time I'm***

here, I feel like I'm failing in the love department. I need your grace because I can't do it on my own.

Failure shows up in all sorts of shapes and sizes, doesn't it? Sometimes it's glaringly public and no one can miss it. At other times, it's quite personal and private, and we're the only ones who know what's happening. But in both scenarios, we need to humbly depend on the grace of our competent God and trust him to supply what we need to live a life that honors him.

As Henry discovered, loving his father proved to be more difficult than he imagined. After Henry's mom passed away, it fell to him to take care of his father. With no siblings who lived locally, it was just Henry and his dad. On most days, Henry found creative ways to stay out of his father's warpath, but other times, it seemed he could do nothing right.

Henry prayed daily for Alan to come to a saving faith in Jesus. He prayed in the morning. He prayed whenever he was on his way to help out. And he felt the need for prayer the most after he had spent time with his father. It was glaringly obvious that Alan was a broken and embittered man. Henry knew that unless Jesus got a hold of his dad's heart, nothing would ever change.

So Henry started to approach the challenging situation from an eternal perspective, and it made all the difference. Instead of responding to his father's hurtful and unkind remarks with more of the same, Henry asked the Lord for fresh insight on how to love his dad. He even changed the way he prayed for his father. No longer were his prayers filled with petitions for God to put his dad in a good mood or to incline him to treat Henry with a civil tongue. Instead, Henry now prayed for God to have mercy on his father and to give him a seeking heart. He begged the Lord to soften his father's hardened heart and asked the Holy Spirit to show his dad that he needed a savior.

Although nothing about the situation improved from Henry's perspective once he changed the way he chose to pray, he did recognize that he himself started to change. He now viewed his dad with a more compassionate heart, which in turn softened the way he talked to him. Henry still felt like a failure in his heart from time to time, but when he did, he ran to the Lord for the grace and mercy he needed in that moment. God always supplied exactly the grace and the strength he required to love and serve his father. For that alone, he gave thanks.

Take-away Action Thought

When I feel like a failure, I will go to this passage of Scripture in Hebrews and meditate on its powerful truth. No matter my circumstances, when I cry to the Lord for help and boldly ask, he will give me mercy and grace in my time of need.

My Heart's Cry to You, O Lord

Father, I'm feeling like such a failure again. It seems like I can handle this challenging situation for a few days, and then something (or someone) sets me off and I'm tempted to respond with the same anger directed at me. My whole being feels upset and frustrated because I'm trying my best to love and serve this person. Please help me to reframe this situation from an eternal perspective. I know that as I view my loved one and this situation from that vantage point, I'll see it differently. Give me the grace to be compassionate, kind, and loving. Help me to remember to boldly run to your throne in my times of need so that I can receive the mercy and grace you have promised me. Amen.

Practicing Grace & Gratitude

1. *Grace & gratitude from God.* "For we do not have a high priest who is unable to empathize with our weaknesses." Each day this week, I'll read one story from the Gospels that tells how Jesus showed compassion and kindness to others even when they mistreated or wronged him.
2. *Grace & gratitude in me.* "Let us then approach God's throne of grace with confidence." Every evening before bedtime this week, I will pray about specific worries or fears I may be battling. I'll bring each one before God and ask for his promised grace.
3. *Grace & gratitude in life.* "So that we may receive mercy and find grace to help us in our time of need." This week I'll spend a few moments every day writing in my journal and listing prayer requests for those challenges in which I need a fresh eternal perspective.

Chapter 9

Practicing Grace & Gratitude in the Home

But godliness with contentment is great gain. For we brought nothing into the world, and we can take nothing out of it. But if we have food and clothing, we will be content with that.

1 Timothy 6:6–8

Who else but a Christian can thank someone for a good meal, a good time, or a good effort, knowing that this has not just been a gift to us from another person but ultimately comes from the living God? I love knowing that He cares and provides for me, not just air to breathe and food to eat, but countless extras that simply flow from His generous heart.

Nancy Leigh DeMoss

Amanda sat at her kitchen table, scrolling through her local online group's announcements for this week's garage and estate sales. To everyone who knew her, Amanda was the "Second-Hand Sales Queen." If there was a deal to be had, she would ferret it out. She was terrific at making the most of sales and coupons and saved considerable amounts of money each month on literally every purchase she made.

One would assume that Amanda's husband Jace would be thrilled with his wife's thriftiness—but he wasn't. In fact, Amanda's constant spending often led to arguments between the two of them. Amanda couldn't understand why her husband would complain about this. After all, when she compared her buying to that of her family and friends, her expenditures always added up much lower than theirs. She didn't understand Jace's issue with her deal hunting because she consistently stayed under their allocated budgeted amounts in every area.

Jace, however, believed that Amanda was missing the bigger picture: that of the more comprehensive and eternal matter of the heart. He had tried to explain to his wife that he was proud of her money-saving savvy. On the other hand, he believed that Amanda struggled with being content with what she had in a material sense. From his point of view, Amanda was constantly looking for something new, different, and better. And because she was so good at shopping, she almost always found what she was looking for.

Jace took issue not with the amount of money Amanda spent, but with the heart attitude that fueled her constant spending. Things came to a head after Amanda arrived home on a Saturday afternoon with yet another trunk load of goods she just couldn't pass up. Jace took Amanda by the hand and sat her down for a long heart-to-heart. "Amanda, I love you, and I am so proud of the way you manage our budget. But I'm asking you to stop spending for a while. I want you to think hard and pray about why you feel the need to keep buying things we don't need. Please ask yourself if there's a deeper reason why you feel compelled to constantly buy and replace what we already have when God has blessed us with so much already."

Amanda didn't say anything. Truthfully, God had already been nudging her to ask the same questions of herself. She agreed to cease spending for the time being. Instead, she decided to invest that time seeking what the Lord would have her do instead of searching out that next best deal.

Have you ever found yourself feeling like Amanda? Always wishing and longing for something newer, different, or better than what you already have? Have you wanted something different than what God has already blessed you with? I have. Maybe not today. Maybe not last week or last month. But I can recall perusing catalogs or surfing online (just yesterday!) when I didn't even need anything. I was simply window-shopping, wasting time, or seeking to distract myself from the world and its woes.

Like Amanda, I can fall for the "new and improved" version right along with everyone else. The older I get, however, the more I feel Paul's words to Timothy piercing my heart and mind: "But godliness with contentment is great gain. For we brought nothing into the world, and we can take nothing out of it. But if we have food and clothing, we will be content with that" (1 Tim. 6:6–8). Honestly, it stops me cold. I have to ask myself, "Do I really need this?" Perhaps the more telling and honest question is this, "What need do I truly believe buying this item will supply?"

I fear that in our affluent and materialistic society, we too often give way to the common temptation to salve our emotional woes by using our purchasing power. Even if we are exceptionally money savvy, like Amanda, and always stick to our budget, should we be buying something if we don't really need it? There is ample biblical support for nurturing a grateful, contented heart rather than giving way to the world's temporary-at-best method of securing happiness and fulfillment. In fact, when we choose to hone our attitude of gratitude and give thanks for what God has blessed us with, we will not only discover those common graces bestowed on all of humanity, but our eyes will be opened to the special blessings God has given each of us individually. May we learn the value of godliness and contentment today so that our tomorrows may be free to love that which will count for eternity.

Take-away Action Thought

When I feel the urge to look for happiness or fulfillment in material goods, I will resist that temptation. Instead of buying something I don't need, I'll see how I can help others who really do have needs—like food, clothing, medicine, and safe shelter. I'll prayerfully do this by connecting with my local food pantry, church, or any of the many Christian aid organizations around the world.

My Heart's Cry to You, O Lord

Father, I have been struggling with a lack of contentment. I feel out of sorts in so many ways, and I know that buying something isn't going to change the condition of my heart. I need to turn toward you, read your word, and allow its powerful truth to permeate my thinking. Please help me to set my heart upon what lasts for all eternity: your word and people's souls. Give me wisdom. Give me a heart set on godliness and contentment. Help me to focus on the real needs of others instead of my unnecessary wants. Amen.

Practicing Grace & Gratitude

1. ***Grace & gratitude from God.*** "But godliness with contentment is great gain." I will spend intentional time this week writing down everything I can think of for which I am grateful. From material goods, to relationships, to health, to my salvation, I'll give thanks for all God's generous blessings.

2. ***Grace & gratitude in me.*** "But if we have food and clothing, we will be content with that." As I spend time in prayer this week, I will ask the Lord to reveal to me any areas of discontent that create turmoil within my heart. As I discover where I am placing material desires above my love for the Lord, I'll confess these sins and ask him to help me hone a more thankful, grateful heart.

3. ***Grace & gratitude in life.*** "For we brought nothing into the world, and we can take nothing out of it." As I consider my tendency to soothe my wounded heart by buying unnecessarily, I will ask the Lord to help me to think outside of myself. I will brainstorm how I might use my money to make an impact for eternity by investing in missions and organizations that help the needy, and by giving generously to others as needs arise.

Chapter 10

Practicing Grace & Gratitude in the Workplace

The Sovereign Lord has given me a well-
instructed tongue,
to know the word that sustains the weary.
He wakens me morning by morning,
wakens my ear to listen like one being
instructed.

Isaiah 50:4

We get up every morning and act upon what is to come, and because what is to come is sure, we know that our labor in God's name is never in vain. So we wait and act. We wait and work. We wait and fight. We wait and conquer. We wait and proclaim. We wait and run. We wait and sacrifice. We wait and give. We wait and worship. Waiting on God is an action based on confident assurance of grace to come.

Paul David Tripp

Ella took a deep breath and let it out slowly before she entered her office. Silently, she prayed that God would give her just the right words to effectively encourage her newest counseling client to stop cutting herself as a habit of self-harm. The growing number of teenagers she met with weekly who were resorting to this dangerous habit to cope with their anxiety and stress was increasingly distressing to her.

Ella sat down at her desk and began reviewing her notes from fourteen-year-old Morgan's last session. Carefully, she reread the comments she had recorded alongside Morgan's responses to her questions. *Oh,* she thought, *to go back to the days when the most destructive acts I ever witnessed within these four walls were kids getting into minor verbal confrontations with their peers. Now all I seem to hear are accounts of life-threatening choices of substance abuse, self-harm, and suicide.*

Ella sighed again. *Lord, help me!* she prayed. *Please give me your words to help direct Morgan away from hurting herself just so she can feel something other than numbness. Sometimes I wonder if I'm making any difference at all. Help me to keep communicating your truth and love to these wounded ones and be thankful you've placed me here to serve them.*

Ella began jotting down specific questions she wanted to discuss with Morgan that day. From long counseling experience, she had become adept at reading her young clients' expressions, and she knew by now just how and when to press a little further to get them to open up. It was all about baby steps. One question, one honest response—that's how she built trust. Ella knew that if she could get Morgan to take a closer look at why she felt compelled to cut herself, then they would have a stepping stone for moving her out of that harmful place.

Prepped and ready for her appointment, Ella pulled out her private journal and spent the next ten minutes listing every bit of positive progress she could think of that related to her clients. She had learned to be proactive about identifying all the good God was doing in these troubled young lives, be it big or small. For her own sake, Ella recorded every tiny step of hope and progress she witnessed taking place. She never wanted to give up on any of her clients, so she learned to give thanks for even the slimmest signs of change. Ella was determined to live in confident assurance of grace to come.

Like Ella, we must choose our attitude and response to the difficulties that surround us. The day-to-day challenges we face may never disappear—in fact, as in Ella's workplace scenario, their severity may actually increase over time. But as Ella learned to remind herself every time she grew weary of trying to fight the spiritual, mental, and emotional battles of the ones in her charge, God is the only one who effectively rescues and changes us from the inside out.

She learned to give thanks to God for every client in whom she had the privilege to invest. She truly lived a confident assurance that it is God alone who equipped her to speak into the lives of these young people. As she developed the daily discipline of identifying and giving thanks for every work of grace God displayed in their lives, her own spirit soared.

Was it challenging for Ella when she didn't see any progress in her clients? Absolutely. Like the rest of us, she fought a real battle against discouragement when nothing in the visible world reassured her that her words and compassion were making any difference. But Ella refused to linger in that place of discouragement. Instead, she prayed for God's sustaining grace to help her be patient. The change Ella hoped and prayed for might not present itself in her desired timeline, or even in her lifetime.

But her confidence wasn't measured in seeing results in the now. She was strengthening her spiritual muscles to serve God and others over the long distance of all of life's ups and downs.

Ella had to confront and face those obstacles that threaten to render her weak and ineffective. And she did so by relying on God to supply her with the grace she needed at each moment of the day. At the same time, she learned to identify the good God was doing and give him thanks. Only then was she able to leave work matters at work and walk away each afternoon in confident assurance of grace to come.

Take-away Action Thought

When I am tempted to give up because I don't believe I'm making any difference in the lives of those with whom I'm working, I will turn to God and ask him for renewed strength and the grace-filled discernment to see the good he is doing behind the scenes.

My Heart's Cry to You, O Lord

Father, I had another difficult and discouraging morning. I didn't think I could handle one more heartbreaking story from those I counsel. I want them to turn their hearts and their pain over to you. But they are so wounded, it's taking a long time to build trust with me. Please give me the words that will bridge the gap between us. Help them to understand that I only want what is best for them. Give me your divine wisdom and understanding to reach each of these hurting ones. And help me to identify the good that you are doing in each of their lives through the gracious work of the Holy Spirit. Amen.

Practicing Grace & Gratitude

1. *Grace & gratitude from God.* "The Sovereign LORD has given me a well-instructed tongue, to know the word that sustains the weary." When my workday has ended, I will spend a few minutes reflecting on the conversations God has allowed me to take part in. I will pray for each person I spoke with according to their most pressing need.
2. *Grace & gratitude in me.* "He wakens me morning by morning." Each morning this week, I won't get out of bed until I've thanked the Lord for five specific blessings for which I am grateful.
3. *Grace & gratitude in life.* "He wakens my ear to listen like one being instructed." My mealtime prayers will include a request that God will help me become a better listener to both him and others. As I learn to be still and truly hear what others are saying, I will gain a better understanding of their deepest needs. This will enable me then to pray for them specifically, giving thanks that I can intercede on their behalf.

Chapter 11

Practicing Grace & Gratitude in Our Churches

Because of the Lord's great love we are not
consumed,
for his compassions never fail.
They are new every morning;
great is your faithfulness.
I say to myself, "The LORD is my portion;
therefore I will wait for him."

Lamentations 3:22–24

There are fresh mercies for you today, form fitted for all the things you will face, both those that you know about and may worry about, and those that you don't know about yet. God's mercy isn't generic. It is personal grace, situational care, and concrete help. It meets you right where you are and gives you just what you need. Yes, this side of forever can be hard, but you're not alone; you've been given sturdy love and new morning mercies—just what you need right here, right now.

Paul David Tripp

Jessica opened her e-mail to find a note from her church's adult ministry pastor, who was letting her know about the changes they were making in the women's ministry department. She was shocked to learn that the single mom's ministry she had spearheaded years ago was being put on hold for the time being while the elders and deacons decided on a few of the logistics.

"What!" she exclaimed aloud to no one but herself. Years ago, when she was raising her own children by herself, she had depended on this ministry. Since she had started leading it, many of the single moms in her church had told her several times just how crucial this ministry had been for them. They counted on it for assistance with their housing, cars, and a whole list of other necessities. How could the church just put it on hold? "This isn't right," she cried. "I'll e-mail Ben right back and tell him how vital this ministry has been to the women in this church and their children."

But as she prepared to send off an impassioned, hurried response to Ben's lengthy note, Jessica stopped herself. ***Wait. Reread that e-mail before you send off some emotional reply.*** She remembered the last time she had replied to one of Ben's messages without stopping to fully read his message. She had immediately been filled with regret and embarrassment after she realized she should have taken more time to study his courteous and thorough guidelines for her new ministry. Even though she was all alone in her office, her face turned bright crimson at the memory.

I sure don't want to repeat my mistakes! Jessica chided herself for her habitual auto-response of impatience. ***I need to take a deep breath, reread the e-mail, and then jot down my thoughts and concerns. And then I should pray before doing anything else.*** "Lord," she prayed aloud. "You know how much this ministry to single moms has meant to me personally. Now,

I want to help those who are in the position I once was—those who need help from every angle. When the time is right, help me to respond with a gracious and grateful spirit. After all, this is your ministry, not mine."

Ministering to others is a wonderfully fulfilling exercise of the grace and gifts given to us by God. He places within our hearts and minds a desire to serve, love, and meet the needs of others. And yet living in the real world means that we will face difficulties and challenges that threaten to be our undoing. Thus, we need, as Paul Tripp so eloquently writes, "sturdy love and new morning mercies" to handle these unwelcome obstacles.

As we learn to discipline ourselves from overreacting to unwanted changes or unexpected developments, we can choose to make grace-filled gratitude our default response. Jessica was learning this very lesson when she stopped herself from reacting emotionally to the news of her single moms' ministry being put "on hold." Naturally, as a single mom herself, she had a personal investment in this much-needed ministry. But as she remembered just in time, it's never wise to respond emotionally without having first calmed down and prayed about the situation.

Jessica also understood that all ministries belong to God. Sure, we might initiate a particular event or lay out details for meeting specific needs, but God is ultimately sovereign over our lives, our ministries, and everything we have been given. This awareness helped Jessica step back and calm down emotionally. She recognized that if God wanted a ministry to succeed, then it would!

Our gifts and talents may open a door for us to serve in the church, but only our humility, openness to change, and teachability will allow our service to flourish. Truly, we need the wise input and perspective of others to help strengthen, broaden, and enrich whatever we put our hearts and hands to serve.

Take-away Action Thought

When I feel upset or discouraged because the ministry I'm involved in isn't working out as I had planned or hoped, I'll step back from being emotional about it and pray. I'll take time to quiet my heart and read the book of Proverbs for wisdom in living a godly life.

My Heart's Cry to You, O Lord

Father, help me to exercise self-control regarding my emotional responses when it comes to protecting "my" ministry. You know that my heart wants to serve my church family in the most efficient way possible. Give me a humble and teachable spirit so that I don't react defensively to others' suggestions. Help me remember that everything in this world, including me and my work in the church, belongs to you to do with as you please. Thank you for the opportunity to give back to others as I was so generously given to in the past. I am grateful for the chance to love and serve your people. Amen.

Practicing Grace & Gratitude

1. *Grace & gratitude from God.* "Because of the Lord's great love we are not consumed, for his compassions

never fail." Each evening this week, I will list five of God's compassions toward me on that day. Then I'll spend time giving thanks to him for each one and how it enriched my day.

2. *Grace & gratitude in me.* "I say to myself, 'The Lord is my portion; therefore I will wait for him.' " Each morning this week, I will take time to say a prayer for humility, wisdom, and teachability so that my attitude is ready to respond appropriately to any challenges or difficulties I may face that day.

3. *Grace & gratitude in life.* "They are new every morning; great is your faithfulness." This week, I will spend time doing a word search of verses in the Bible that talk about "faithfulness." I'll write down a few of these passages to carry with me throughout my day so that I can reflect and remember God's perfect provision designed just for me.

Chapter 12

Practicing Grace & Gratitude in Our Neighborhoods

"Love your enemies, do good to those who hate you, bless those who curse you, pray for those who mistreat you. If someone slaps you on one cheek, turn to them the other also. If someone takes your coat, do not withhold your shirt from them. Give to everyone who asks you, and if anyone takes what belongs to you, do not demand it back. Do to others as you would have them do to you."

Luke 6:27–31

How can you and I not be grateful for God's patience with us? He doesn't demand of us instant maturity. He doesn't require that we get it right quickly. He doesn't teach us a lesson just once. He comes to us in situation after situation, each controlled by his sovereign grace, each designed to be a tool of transformation, and he works on the same things again and again.

Paul David Tripp

Married for over fifty years, Sally and Derek had a daily ritual that included taking their two golden retrievers on a long walk through their neighborhood. Both were avid outdoors people, and they frequently enjoyed stopping along their walking route to chat with longtime neighbors who were outside caring for their lawns, gardening, or simply enjoying the weather. So when Sally unexpectedly began to beg off their daily trek, Derek felt a bit dismayed and confused.

After she had refused to walk for several consecutive days without any obvious good reason, Derek finally asked her point blank, "Why don't you want to walk through the neighborhood anymore? Did something happen I'm not aware of?"

Sally shook her head. "No, nothing happened. It's just that every time we walk by Carl's house, I have to avert my eyes because I get so upset. It's those hateful signs he put up on his front lawn. He's causing a big problem with the other neighbors too, and he doesn't care."

Derek hadn't even noticed these signs! Before she said anything else, he indicated to her to wait and then proceeded to take one of the dogs to go off to investigate. Sure enough, Sally had been correct. When Derek spotted the signs in Carl's yard, he cringed. ***No wonder Sally and other neighbors are upset! These signs are hateful and certainly won't do any good toward creating an atmosphere of neighborly love.***

Sally had been watching him from the window, so she met him the moment he came back in. "Well? What do you think?" she asked. "Am I right?"

"Yes, you're right," he said unleashing the dog. "Those signs aren't going to win Carl any good neighbor awards from anyone, that's for sure. But giving up our walks to avoid going by his house isn't the answer, Sally. We know Carl's background. We also know he put up these signs out of frustration. He doesn't know any better . . . but we do." Derek looked at Sally meaningfully and then continued, "Even though what Carl is doing is offensive, hateful even, we're called to overcome evil with good and to love him. We may be the only Christians Carl ever comes into contact with. We need to reach out in love to him. Especially now."

"I know you're right," she responded. "I just wish my feelings would catch up with what I know is the right thing to do. Carl is one tough man to love."

"Yes, I know. But we need to love Carl now and not wait for our emotions to get with the program."

When someone offends us, whether they did it intentionally or not, God's word tells us how we should respond. In simple terms, we are to love our enemies. We are to go beyond merely being courteous and kind. As believers, we must purposefully do good to these difficult folks, bless them, pray for them, and treat them as we would want to be treated. That's a high calling indeed.

From Sally and Derek's point of view, their neighbor gave them lots of reasons to turn away from him. But as Derek reminded his wife, Carl had his own reasons for his dubious behavior, which he used to justify his actions whenever he was confronted. Although Derek and Sally couldn't persuade Carl to take a different stance on issues about which he was passionate, they could rise above his divisive behavior by simply focusing on loving him.

There is no greater power on earth than the supernatural, Spirit-infused, ability to love one's enemies. Regardless of how much (or how frequently) Sally and Derek might disagree with Carl, their marching orders were to love, bless, serve, and pray for him. When we experience the sting of rejection, unkindness, or anger from others who live and believe differently than we do, we as Christians have no other choice than to respond in love. Difficult? Yes, but as we obey our Lord by offering grace-filled responses, God's enabling grace comes into play in our attitudes, our words, our actions, and most importantly, within our own hearts. As we choose to honor God in these challenging life scenarios, not only will we be given grace from above, but our hearts will also soften toward these who oppose us. And for that, we can be eternally grateful.

Take-away Action Thought

When I'm tempted to give way to unrighteous anger, I will step away from the volatile situation and get to a quiet, solitary place to seek the Lord's wisdom on how to respond. I'll take all the time it requires for me to calm down, and I'll spend time reading through the book of Proverbs to gain fresh insight on this troubling encounter.

My Heart's Cry to You, O Lord

Father, I'm so upset right now I can hardly focus on anything. I feel angry and frustrated with this situation because I can't change or control it. Please help me to remember that you're the one in control over everything that happens in this world. Help me to place my confidence in you, rather than get distracted by troubling circumstances. You alone can change individuals' hearts and minds. Give me the wisdom and grace to accept that truth and be content with doing my best to overcome evil with good by loving, blessing, and praying for those who are difficult to love. Amen.

Practicing Grace & Gratitude

1. *Grace & gratitude from God.* "Love your enemies, do good to those who hate you, bless those who curse you." This week, I will spend time searching the book of Proverbs for verses about wise and godly living. I'll write down those verses that are especially pertinent and meaningful to me in this situation.
2. *Grace & gratitude in me.* "Pray for those who mistreat you." Each evening, I'll devote time to pray specifically for anyone I'm struggling to love and serve. I'll spend extra time praying for anyone I view as my enemy.
3. *Grace & gratitude in life.* "Do to others as you would have them do to you." Each day this week, I'll choose one difficult person in my life to serve and bless with a kind note or some sort of tangible gift to encourage them. I'll ask God to show me how I can communicate to these individuals that I care for them deeply.

Chapter 13

Practicing Grace & Gratitude with Our Families

The end of all things is near. Therefore be alert and of sober mind so that you may pray. Above all, love each other deeply, because love covers over a multitude of sins.

1 Peter 4:7–8

Experiences labeled as the worst things that ever happened, over time become some of the best. That's because God uses the painful, difficult experiences of life for our ultimate good.

Randy Alcorn

Noah felt fidgety as he sat holding the printed memorial card with his grandfather's picture and life summary in his hands. Earlier that week, Grandpa Mack died suddenly from a massive heart attack. When Noah heard the news, he immediately drove back home from his out-of-state-college and spent the last three days helping his mom and dad prepare for the funeral.

As the family's only grandson, Noah saw Grandpa Mack as a wonderful and kind man. Noah had countless memories of his grandfather taking him on fishing trips during the summer months and skiing in the winter. Grandpa was a hands-on kind of man, and Noah adored him. Whenever he received an invitation to spend time with his grandpa, he always jumped at the chance.

It wasn't until Grandpa Mack passed away and Noah and his parents spent hours shuffling through old family photos that Noah first got the impression that his dad, Tom, didn't have the same good feelings toward Grandpa Mack. Noah would never forget the look on his father's face when he pulled out photos of Noah and Grandpa Mack holding a string line of small mouth bass and smiling from ear to ear. As his dad held the pictures and looked at them, he began crying.

Stunned by his father's emotional reaction, Noah assumed he was grieving his loss. But when he tried to console him with some kind words about what a great dad Grandpa Mack must have been, Tom simply shook his head.

"I never wanted you to think poorly of your grandfather, Noah," Tom began, "but he was a very different man when I was growing up. We often were on the wrong side of his temper—and his belt. He changed a lot after I left home and even more after your grandmother died. I was thankful that he finally learned how to love, but my memories of him are anything but sweet."

Noah didn't know what to say, so he sat in silence, trying to work through this devastating revelation about his beloved grandfather.

On the morning of the funeral, Noah wondered what Tom would say about his dad when it was his turn to speak. Noah wouldn't blame him if he chose not to get up to talk before their gathering of family and friends. But what he said astounded Noah.

"My dad's passing has brought back many memories to me and to our family this past week. One of the most important roles my father played was that of a dedicated and committed grandfather to my son. I'll always be thankful that Noah has such a treasure of memories to reflect back on and all lessons he learned from my father. My father understood the value of being involved with his grandson, and for that, I'm grateful."

Noah sat stunned. Although he now knew how his grandfather had treated his dad, he was amazed that he didn't even mention his own personal pain and disappointment. Instead, he chose to highlight to others only what Grandpa Mack did right. With tears in his own eyes, Noah felt proud of his father. He knew how much that brief eulogy had cost him personally. Noah never forgot his father's gracious example of covering over in love his grandfather's failings as a parent.

Love does cover a multitude of sins. It can forgive the failings and disappointments, as well as any mixture of minor irritation and personal upset. It can choose to highlight the best in a person rather than dwell on their worst mistakes and poor choices. And that is exactly what God calls each of us to do today.

Like Tom, most of us have probably experienced the stinging pain of when someone we love has not loved us well. The degree of the hurt may be different for everyone, but because we live in a broken world, pain and suffering comes to every person. We can choose, as Tom did, to look for the redeeming qualities of those in our family. Or we can hang onto personal injuries and remain mired in resentment and bitterness.

Tom chose the best thing. He chose to forgive his errant father for all the pain he caused Tom as a young child. He chose to look for the good in his father's life. And he found it. While nothing could undo the past or rewind lost opportunities, Tom knew that God wanted him to focus on his father's later years, when he did his best to treat his grandson with love.

In making this choice, Tom was freed from the inside out to reflect back on his own childhood from a perspective that enabled him to learn from his painful experience and to not repeat his father's actions with his own son. Having grown up feeling unloved, Tom relied on God's grace to parent differently than his father had. He frequently went to the Lord in prayer, asking him for wisdom and understanding to be the man and the father that God intended.

Tom understood that sometimes the worst experiences can be transformed into the best when God takes the lead and shows us how to overcome evil with good. And in the process, we are healed, set free, and equipped to love others more selflessly.

Take-away Action Thought

When the pain from my past threatens to overwhelm me, I will ask God to show me how he is redeeming this personal pain into opportunities to love and serve others.

My Heart's Cry to You, O Lord

Father, I have been revisiting my past too much lately. The more I replay those painful events, the lower I sink emotionally. Right now, I'm struggling with anger against someone who hurt me deeply. Please help me to forgive and begin praying for this person. Help me to see something good in them so that I might be able to bridge the gap between us and begin to rebuild our relationship. Let me never forget that you died on a cross to save me from my sins and that I need forgiveness too. Amen.

Practicing Grace & Gratitude

1. *Grace & gratitude from God.* "The end of all things is near. Therefore be alert and of sober mind so that you may pray." As I pray this week, I will focus on seeing my life through the lens of eternity. I'll ask God to help me keep sharing the gospel and making disciples my primary purpose and not allow myself to get sidetracked by small insults and injuries.
2. *Grace & gratitude in me.* "Above all, love each other deeply." Each day this week, I will choose a different family member to love in a special way—whether through acts of service, a small gift, or words of encouragement.
3. *Grace & gratitude in life.* "Love covers over a multitude of sins." In my prayer journal, I'll write down anyone I have failed to forgive. And after confessing this sin, I'll commit to praying for each person's spiritual welfare and personal well-being this week.

Chapter 14

Practicing Grace & Gratitude with Our Friends

Love is patient, love is kind. It does not envy, it does not boast, it is not proud. It does not dishonor others, it is not self-seeking, it is not easily angered, it keeps no record of wrongs. Love does not delight in evil but rejoices with the truth. It always protects, always trusts, always hopes, always perseveres.

1 Corinthians 13:4–7

When we get hurt, no matter how serious the offense or how deep the wound, God has grace available to help us deal with the offense and forgive the offender. At that point, we have one of two choices: We can acknowledge our need and humbly reach out to Him for His grace to forgive and release the offender. Or we can resist Him, fail to receive His grace, and hold on to the hurt. If we take the latter course, bitterness will take root in the soil of our hearts. In time, that root will spring up and cause trouble for us and for others around us who will be affected by our unforgiving spirit.

Nancy Leigh DeMoss

Forgive me, Lord, for having to come to you again with my complaining heart. I know I struggle with being oversensitive, but I'm feeling so conflicted by Kimmy's harsh words about my son. Sometimes I wonder if she even considers me a friend at all when she is so critical of Chase. Help me to sort out all these confusing emotions and give me the wisdom to know how to be the kind of friend she needs, even if Kimmy can't reciprocate that love toward me." Jill lifted her head, opened her eyes, and sighed deeply. She was doing her best to work through her most recent hurtful conversation with her friend.

Both women attended the same church, and their sons were in the same Sunday school class, so they saw each other at least twice every week. Jill had been paired up with Kimmy as parent helpers in their children's classroom. Each time they worked together, it seemed as though Kimmy found some reason to criticize Chase's behavior. Jill was deeply stung by Kimmy's remarks. She repeatedly reprimanded Jill's son Chase for minor infractions while her own son Kyle hardly ever behaved at all. Jill was not only puzzled by this contradiction but hurt too.

Why did Kimmy feel so comfortable correcting someone else's child when her own son was consistently out of control or raging against the other children? It made no sense to Jill, so she prayed. When the next Sunday service rolled around and Jill and Kimmy were to serve together, Jill prepared herself both prayerfully and practically. She knew that Kimmy loved sunflowers, so she stopped at the floral department while grocery shopping and picked out the biggest bouquet on display. Armed with a prayer-filled, grace-infused attitude, Jill entered the Sunday school classroom ready to do one thing: look for fresh ways to love and better understand Kimmy. Rather than focus on her own disappointment and hurt feelings, Jill chose the higher path: to forgive her but also let her know how she was feeling. Seeing the grateful expression on Kimmy's face when Jill presented her with the flowers, she felt a surge of thankfulness herself. When they sat down to finally have that honest conversation, Jill had a renewed hope for their friendship.

When we seek to love others more than we seek to be loved by them, God provides us with grace from above to love unconditionally—even when someone is being cruel or unkind. When we concentrate on doing our part in the friendship equation rather than placing demands on others, we are free indeed. This is not to say that when we are sinned against, either in attitude or action, we should blindly accept the situation. But we first need to consider what's in our own hearts before we can have an honest conversation (if possible) with the one who caused the hurt.

First Corinthians 13 clearly lays out what genuine love toward others looks like in the real world:

> Love is patient, love is kind. It does not envy, it does not boast, it is not proud. It does not dishonor others, it is not self-seeking, it is not easily angered, it keeps no record of wrongs. Love does not delight in evil but rejoices with the truth. It always protects, always trusts, always hopes, always perseveres.

From beginning to end, God describes with stunning, comprehensive clarity what loving others entails.

God knows we are going to be faced with painful and disappointing situations with those we consider friends. Which is why, I believe, he places so much emphasis on the right way to respond to our offenders. This passage doesn't leave room for us to respond to evil with more evil, seek revenge, enact a plan to get even, or even stay angry. No, God warns us that when we choose the path of anger and bitterness, we aren't the only ones who end up suffering for our sinful response. We infect everyone around us, because we can't contain or merely internalize our disobedience. It spills out of us both consciously and unconsciously. Serious stuff indeed!

God not only anticipates the problems we will face, but he also provides the perfect response for us to embrace. We cannot overcome evil with good from a pure heart unless the Holy Spirit gives us the grace to do so. When we rely on his abiding grace to obey in love, our hearts will soar in gratitude to God for his wisdom, power, and might that fully equip us to represent the love of Jesus to one and all.

Take-away Action Thought

When I feel hurt by a friend's words or actions toward me, I'll memorize this passage in 1 Corinthians 13 about what genuine love looks like in the real world. Then I'll spend time praying for my friend and our troubling situation.

My Heart's Cry to You, O Lord

Father, I'm feeling such sadness and disappointment with my friend. I can't seem to stop replaying the hurtful words she said to me. I don't understand why she is seemingly trying to hurt me with her unkind comments. I'm trying to respond in ways that are loving, even though I feel confused by her behavior. Please give me the grace to continue to love her unconditionally and the wisdom to know how to deal with it. I want to show grace toward her, and I rely on you to show me how to navigate through this hurtful place. I know you will show me the right path to take. Amen.

Practicing Grace & Gratitude

1. ***Grace & gratitude from God.*** "[Love] always protects, always trusts, always hopes, always perseveres." This week, I'll make a list of everything about my friend for which I am sincerely grateful. I'll write down everything that is positive and God-honoring. Then I will spend time each day praying for my friend's spiritual welfare.
2. ***Grace & gratitude in me.*** "[Love] does not dishonor others, it is not self-seeking, it is not easily angered, it keeps no record of wrongs." Each day, I prayerfully ask the Lord if there is anyone I'm holding anger and bitterness toward. As needed, I will confess my sinful attitude, ask the Lord for the renewed love for each of these individuals, and then commit to pray for them daily.
3. ***Grace & gratitude in life.*** "Love is patient, love is kind. It does not envy, it does not boast, it is not proud." At the end of the week, I'll spend time thinking about my interactions with others, while being mindful of my heart attitude in each situation. I'll ask the Lord to reveal to me if I was exhibiting impatience, unkindness, jealousy, or pride with my words, my actions, or even more subtly within my heart.

Chapter 15

Practicing Grace & Gratitude with Our Acquaintances

As God's chosen people, holy and dearly loved, clothe yourselves with compassion, kindness, humility, gentleness and patience. Bear with each other and forgive one another if any of you has a grievance against someone. Forgive as the Lord forgave you. And over all these virtues put on love, which binds them all together in perfect unity.

Colossians 3:12–14

We have been called to represent the King in a way that incarnates him. To incarnate means to embody in human form, to personify. We are his hands, his eyes, his ears, and his mouths. We put flesh and blood to who he is and what he wants for those around us. We are called to make his character and will be seen, heard, and known.

Paul David Tripp

Eve fought against the temptation to complain to her sister Becca about her new neighbor's wandering cats that kept sneaking into her garage whenever she came and went from her home. Eve had lived on the same street for twenty years and never once had a problem with any of her neighbors. In fact, most of her neighbors had become good friends. But a few months ago, her elderly friend Joyce next door passed away and her house went up for sale.

Whoever moves in just won't compare to Joyce, I know, Eve had thought as she eyed the moving truck unloading furniture and household goods one late Saturday. It didn't take her long to discover just how different her new neighbor would be. Landrie was a single woman, and she hadn't been living in her new house for too long before she began neglecting her lawn, her cats, and her fellow neighbors' unwritten code about being neighborly in every sense of the word.

Over the next weeks, Eve listened to each of her surrounding neighbors complain in turn about Landrie's unkempt lawn, her loud music late at night, and her garbage cans that frequently fell over scattering bottles, cans, and debris everywhere. But most of all, she heard her longtime neighbors grouse about Landrie's wandering cats, who seemed to believe the entire street was their personal litter box, and how rude Landrie was to her neighbors when they went to meet and greet her. Eve puzzled over this cranky demeanor that Landrie exhibited to one and all.

While Eve felt the same frustration as her other neighbors over Landrie's defensive attitude, she tried to offer compassion and understanding whenever the topic arose. As a Christian, she knew her neighbors were observing her and her responses, so she tried not to enter into the negative banter. But one evening after a long day, Eve finally reached her boiling point when she drove into her garage only to have two cats drop from the ceiling onto her dashboard. Startled and angry, Eve shooed them out, shut the garage door, and immediately called her sister.

After venting to Becca, Eve waited for her sister to commiserate with her woes. For a while, there was only silence. But then Becca spoke up and said, "Remember how Grandma never said an unkind word about anyone? I'm still aspiring to that. And I know you are too, Sis." Becca paused before adding, "Don't shoot the messenger, but you know I'm right."

Eve took a deep breath. Of course Becca was right. "Message received loud and clear."

"I know how difficult it's been since Landrie moved in but complaining about her is only going to make you feel worse by fueling the fire of your frustration with her. Let's pray and find a way to navigate all these irritations and her impoliteness in a way that honors the Lord and demonstrates to Landrie his love for her."

Choosing the correct biblical response is so important. The words we select, the tone of our voice, and our body language speaks volumes to others. But all the "right" words won't communicate the love we need to express if our hearts aren't in step with the Spirit. Eve desired to keep an open mind and an open heart toward her not-so-neighborly new neighbor. Even though she sorely missed her former wonderful friend and neighbor, Joyce, she was prepared to love Landrie and welcome her warmly.

That is, until Landrie's lack of common courtesy and sensitivity began to dampen Eve's desire to demonstrate unconditional love toward her. All the grousing and complaining from the rest of her neighbors only served to fuel the simmering frustration Eve already felt. But then God did something remarkable. He orchestrated a personal rescue of sorts. God used Eve's sister

Becca to speak truth into her troubled heart by reminding Eve of their godly grandmother's example.

Isn't that just like the Lord to bring another believer to us who will speak the truth we so desperately need to hear? I can remember many times when I struggled to love someone as God would have me do and then another believer was sent my way to challenge me, chastise me, and on occasion, gently rebuke me. And I needed that! We all require a jumpstart of our hearts at times.

When someone rubs us the wrong way, even if they are completely unaware of how their actions are affecting us, it's tempting to turn away from them in anger and irritation. But God tells us to respond differently. Colossians 3 says to "bear with each other and forgive one another if any of you has a grievance against someone." And how are we to accomplish this lofty task? By clothing ourselves "with compassion, kindness, humility, gentleness and patience." Only when our hearts are oriented to love others can we rightly represent our God to a watching world.

Take-away Action Thought

When I begin to feel angry, frustrated, or irritated with someone, I will remove myself from the situation, sit down with my Bible and take time to read carefully through Colossians 3. I'll meditate on this section of Scripture until I feel settled and ready to love intentionally and unconditionally.

My Heart's Cry to You, O Lord

Father, I'm struggling today with my heart attitude toward my neighbor. I thought it would be easy to love her, but I was wrong. It seems like every day, she does something rude and thoughtless, and I find myself becoming angry at her. Please help me to have a tender and loving heart toward her regardless of her actions. Give me the grace to love her unconditionally. Remind me to pray daily for her and help me find creative ways to demonstrate your love for her. Amen.

Practicing Grace & Gratitude

1. *Grace & gratitude from God.* "As God's chosen people, holy and dearly loved, clothe yourselves with compassion, kindness, humility, gentleness and patience." I will memorize this portion of Scripture and recite it throughout the day to remind myself of how God wants me to be clothed in character so that I rightly reflect Jesus' love toward others.
2. *Grace & gratitude in me.* "Bear with each other and forgive one another if any of you has a grievance against someone." Each evening, I will spend some time reflecting on the day and asking the Lord to reveal to me anyone against whom I'm holding a grudge. Then I'll spend time first asking for forgiveness and then praying for these individuals.
3. *Grace & gratitude in life.* "Forgive as the Lord forgave you. And over all these virtues put on love, which binds them all together in perfect unity." Each day this week, I'll ask the Lord to give me creative ways to demonstrate love to those with whom I come into contact.

Chapter 16

An Attitude of Grace-Filled Gratitude Changes Us

"My command is this: Love each other as I have loved you. Greater love has no one than this: to lay down one's life for one's friends. You are my friends if you do what I command. . . . This is my command: Love each other."

John 15:12–14, 17

There's a buzzword used today to describe what takes place when a person adjusts the thought patterns that have become ingrained into his or her emotional makeup. It's called: "attitudinal change." It's a fancy way to say that new behaviors start with new mind-sets. The pathway to personal transformation requires a change in perspective.

Nancy Leigh DeMoss

Bailey sat holding her graduation diploma that had arrived in the mail earlier that morning. She couldn't stop running her finger over the raised emblem at the bottom of the certificate that told the world she had indeed graduated from college with a bachelor's degree. She felt so absolutely content that nothing could ruin this perfect moment for her.

After silently reminiscing a few more minutes about her last four years of sacrifice, self-discipline, and hard work, Bailey carefully tucked her treasured diploma into her desk drawer for safekeeping until she could buy a suitable frame for it. Closing the drawer, she eyed the guest list for her upcoming graduation party. ***It will be so wonderful to celebrate with my friends and family***, she thought wistfully. ***All that hard work has finally paid off and I'm officially done with college!***

As the first person in her family to attend college as well as the first one to graduate with a bachelor's degree, Bailey felt an extra sense of personal accomplishment. She couldn't wait to see her mom and her brothers to show them her official diploma.

Since she had heard back from them on the invitations she sent out, she decided to call her mom to make sure they'd all received them. Her mom confirmed that they had but that none of them could make it to the party. Although it was a short conversation, it was long enough to burst Bailey's party balloon. She hung up the phone with that sickening and familiar feeling of disappointment. She should be used to this by now, but it always hurts. She thought that at least this one time, her mom and brothers would make the effort to come to see her. She couldn't believe that her friends supported her more than her own family. She was so hurt that she was tempted to cancel the party she had been so excited about only minutes earlier.

Completely deflated by her mother's lack of support and disinterest, Bailey plopped down on the sofa and let her tears flow. After a while, her roommate Jordan arrived home and immediately read the room. "You spoke with your mom, didn't you? And let me guess—she isn't coming to your party."

Bailey nodded as she blew her nose. "I'm so upset at myself for getting my hopes up. But we're talking about my graduation.

I really thought this one time my mom might come through and show up. I was wrong."

"Oh, Bailey. We already know your mom has so many personal problems of her own she can hardly care for your brothers. But I get it; I would be disappointed too." Jordan sat down next to her and gave her a much-needed hug. "Listen to me: We are not going to let your mom ruin your celebration. We are going to throw the best graduation party ever!"

Continuing to love those who don't seem to return our love is a risky business sometimes. Unfortunately, some people simply aren't equipped to show love in the way we need them to. This could be due to trauma in their own lives or simply because they choose not to. Accepting the hard truth that one's family may be among those who cannot or will not offer the loving support we need is especially painful, as Bailey discovered over and over again.

Through the years, Bailey believed she had wisely learned to let go of any expectations from her mother, but she hadn't. She continued to hope that one day her mother might recognize her daughter's worth and need and become the mom for which Bailey had always longed. Even as she moved into adulthood, Bailey consistently reached out and demonstrated unconditional love toward her mother. She did as Jesus commanded and loved her mother, despite her mom's refusal to reciprocate that love. This made Bailey wonder how much of that stemmed from her grandmother's struggle with demonstrating any type of emotional love toward her mom and siblings. Bailey understood how difficult a childhood her mom had endured after her father died and her grandmother was left to raise her children alone. Still, Bailey hoped her mom might soften as she grew older.

On the flip side, what Bailey lacked in familial support, she made up for in abundance through her friends. Bailey obeyed God's command to love others and she practiced selflessly putting others' needs before her own, meaning she was well-loved by her friends, her classmates, and her coworkers. What she was also slowly learning to do was to make an "attitudinal change." As she worked on changing her perspective about her family, she began to finally feel free.

Bailey learned to stop putting hopeful expectations into receiving her mother's love in the way she needed. Today, she continues to do her part to express love toward her family, but she wisely recognizes that it is highly unlikely they will ever give back to her in the same measure that she gives. Bailey grew freer from the inside out as she let go of her expectations and allowed God to love her through her faithful friends who saw her for the treasure she was. Bailey often revisited John 15 and found it comforting to know that Jesus was not only her Savior, but he was also her friend.

Take-away Action Thought

When my expectations are dashed and my feelings are hurt because someone I love doesn't demonstrate love toward me, I will tell Jesus how I'm feeling. I will then meditate on John 15:12–14, 17 and give thanks that Jesus calls me his friend.

My Heart's Cry to You, O Lord

Father, I'm feeling so hurt and disappointed. I should know better by now than to expect support from someone who has consistently let me down, but some hope never dies. It will probably always be a longing in my heart to be close to them, even if they don't feel the same way. Please remind me to run to you when I feel this way and to not allow anger or resentment to take root in my heart. I know you command me to love others, and I want to obey you in this, but I need your strength to do it. Pour your abundant grace into my heart so that my desire is to love unconditionally. Amen.

Practicing Grace & Gratitude

1. *Grace & gratitude from God.* "My command is this: Love each other as I have loved you." Day by day, I will be mindful of loving others unconditionally and not allow their behavior toward me to dictate how I treat them. I will remind myself that God expects my obedience and that his grace will help me govern my thoughts and actions, even when I'm disappointed or hurt.
2. *Grace & gratitude in me.* "Greater love has no one than this: to lay down one's life for one's friends." Each evening this week, I'll spend time praying specifically for my family and friends by name. I'll also give thanks for each of them, even if I have an uneasy relationship with them.
3. *Grace & gratitude in life.* "You are my friends if you do what I command. This is my command: Love each other." This week, I'll prayerfully reflect on any past hurts I may be clinging to that hinder me from loving others unconditionally. I'll confess these unloving thoughts and attitudes and look for ways to demonstrate my love and care for each person.

Chapter 17

An Attitude of Grace-Filled Gratitude Stretches Us

Now faith is confidence in what we hope for and assurance about what we do not see. . . . And without faith it is impossible to please God, because anyone who comes to him must believe that he exists and that he rewards those who earnestly seek him.

Hebrews 11:1, 6

He has never failed to honor believing prayer. He may keep you waiting for a while, but delays are not denials. He has often answered a prayer that asked for silver by giving gold. He may have denied earthly treasure, but He has given heavenly riches of ten thousand times the worth, and the suppliant has been more than satisfied with the exchange.

Charles Spurgeon

At 2:00 a.m., Natalie's phone woke her with a start. As she reached for it, her heart began to race. Her twin sister, Nora, must be in labor! Seeing her sister's name on her caller ID, Natalie excitedly answered, "Nora! Is it time? I'll get dressed and meet you at the hospital." With that brief exchange, she tossed the phone on the bed and threw on a sweatshirt and pants. In less than ten minutes, Natalie was out the door and on her way to the hospital where her sister would be giving birth to her third child.

Driving through the sleeping neighborhood, Natalie began to make a mental list of people she needed to contact once she got to the hospital. ***I need to alert our women's prayer team, and I'll text Evan and the boys at the lake house too. Oh, and I need to call Nora's in-laws as well. Lord, help Nora's delivery to go smoothly***, she prayed. ***I'm not sure how much help I'll be since I've never given birth, but I can still be supportive and present.***

As she turned onto the highway, she thought again about that painful season of waiting when she had longed for a child of her own more than anything else. For over five years, Natalie and her husband, Evan, tried unsuccessfully to conceive. Finally, they decided to begin the adoption process, and after waiting for another two years, they received a middle-of-the-night phone call from a social worker who matched newborns with adoptive parents. That one call changed their lives forever: Natalie and Evan became parents to two infant twin boys. She often teased Nora that she got them on a "two for one deal," just like their mom had in giving birth to the two of them.

Natalie smiled at the memory of how God had uniquely chosen to grow their family through adoption. It had been so hard to hang on to hope month after month while trying to conceive. And then it was harder still to wait those two years before she and Evan were able to adopt their boys. Yet looking back, it was worth every moment of waiting and every tear they cried. ***God definitely used this waiting to stretch us spiritually***, she conceded. As she pulled into the hospital parking lot, Natalie turned her thoughts back to the present moment. ***Oh Lord, help me to support and encourage my beautiful sister as she labors to bring forth another blessing from above.***

Each of us has prayed and waited for God to answer. Each of us has also spent time wondering if God has heard our prayers. None of us enjoys the uneasy space between asking and receiving. And yet, as the writer of Hebrews reminds us, God is pleased when we offer our prayers and requests to him believing that he hears us and that he will answer us in his own good time and in his own good way.

Isn't it amazing how Scripture tells us that God wants us to know and believe that he rewards those who seek him? Lest we mistakenly believe this means we will receive blessings of the material kind for simply believing, we must understand that God's greatest blessings are of the spiritual sort. Charles Spurgeon's quotation says it well: "He may have denied earthly treasure, but He has given heavenly riches of ten thousand times the worth, and the suppliant has been more than satisfied with the exchange."

Often, I fear, as Spurgeon says, we ask for silver when God desires to give us gold. We see only the human and material realm before us and pray for what will only satisfy us temporarily rather than eternally. But God—who sees our past, present, and future—tailors his answers to our prayers accordingly. He wisely considers all time and eternity when he answers our prayers with his divine plan in mind.

His eternal purposes come into play even while he has us in the waiting stage because he is busy stretching us, growing us, and remaking us into the image of his dear Son, Jesus. God understands our struggles with delayed answers to our prayers, and he compassionately bestows on us the grace we require to press through the seasons of waiting with a grace-filled, gratitude-infused heart that willingly submits to his perfect plan (and perfect timing) for each of us.

Take-away Action Thought

When I become weary of waiting, I will remind myself that God is working behind the scenes, orchestrating what is good for me and for that which will bring him glory. I will also remind myself that delays are not denials.

My Heart's Cry to You, O Lord

Father, you know I am not good at waiting. I struggle with trying to move things along to suit my timetable instead of patiently accepting your perfect timing and your perfect answer to my prayers. Please help me to learn to trust you to work things out as you know best. Give me the grace I need to place what matters most to me into your loving, faithful hands and to leave even my dearest hope and desires with you. I know that every time I choose to trust you, my inner joy and peace abound. Amen.

Practicing Grace & Gratitude

1. *Grace & gratitude from God.* "Anyone who comes to him must believe that he exists and that he rewards those who earnestly seek him." In prayer this week, I'll focus on giving thanks for the grace God bestows on me to wait on his perfect answer (and timing) in a way that pleases him. I will give thanks even before my prayers are answered, knowing that God desires only what is best for me.

2. ***Grace & gratitude in me.*** "Now faith is confidence in what we hope for and assurance about what we do not see." This week, I'll write down specific instances of when I prayed for something, and God didn't answer right away. I'll recall my thoughts, feelings, and how God stretched me spiritually during the process. Specifically, I'll make note of how, in hindsight, God used those seasons of waiting to grow me.
3. ***Grace & gratitude in life.*** "Without faith it is impossible to please God." This week, I'll do a word study on verses that include "faith" in them. I will read through these texts and write down several to carry with me throughout my week.

Chapter 18

An Attitude of Grace-Filled Gratitude Humbles Us

You who are younger, submit yourselves to your elders. All of you, clothe yourselves with humility toward one another, because, "God opposes the proud but shows favor to the humble." Humble yourselves, therefore, under God's mighty hand, that he may lift you up in due time. Cast all your anxiety on him because he cares for you.

1 Peter 5:5–7

I sighed and you heard me. I wavered and you steadied me. I travelled along the broad way of the world, but you did not desert me.

Augustine

Anna counted her tips and then dropped them into her work satchel before finishing her shift at the breakfast diner where she worked each morning. Happy with the extra cash she made during the early morning rush, Anna hoped that tomorrow she would do as well. ***As long as Elsie is gone on vacation, I will meet my budget***, she told herself. College was expensive. Gas and insurance were expensive too, and Anna needed every extra penny she could earn.

Anna reflected back on more profitable days, before the diner's new morning manager came on the scene. Before Elsie took over the morning shift, Anna always made enough money to cover her expenses and then some. But when Elsie took over the front reception desk, she began giving her friend Nancy the customers ahead of Anna. ***It's not right***, Anna thought. ***Elsie knows she's supposed to take turns splitting tables between us, but she doesn't. I can even calculate the number of tips I've lost since she started managing the morning shift.***

Every morning, Anna fought a mental battle with herself as she walked through the diner's doors to begin her shift. She wanted to be gracious and understanding. She prayed for God to help her to be kind toward Elsie and Nancy, despite how they were taking advantage of her. ***It's because I'm young***, she often thought to herself. ***They think I don't notice what's really going on—but everyone sees it. Even the customers have remarked on it***!

After another long morning at the diner, followed by her classes, Anna was grateful to drop her bag and books on the table and settle in for the evening. Because of her early morning schedule, she chose to spend her time with God at night. She would fix a simple meal and sit down to eat with her Bible open before her. Anna loved unpacking her busy days with the Lord, interspersing mealtime with prayer time.

On this particular evening, as Anna was working through 1 Peter 5, she found herself rereading verses 5–7. "Oh Lord," she prayed aloud. "Please clothe me with a spirit of humility. I need your favor and grace in a big way to handle the challenges at work. Help me to be respectful and to trust in your perfect provision for me. I can't change the situation at work, but I can honor you by choosing to respond humbly and respectfully."

Who among us hasn't faced situations where favoritism was shown to others? As a young adult worker, I recall observing a supervisor blatantly ignore the poor work ethic of a favored coworker while the rest of us labored hard. Admittedly, it was difficult to watch or accept. Like Anna's experience, this discouraging scenario continued for months until a new supervisor replaced the former one.

I've thought long and hard about that unfair situation and wondered if I might handle it differently now that I'm older. I recall feeling just as Anna felt; and though it took me longer to get a handle on it, I also went to the Lord and began to pray for his wisdom and guidance. I remember asking him to help me to overcome evil with good. It then became my mission to show kindness, compassion, and respect to this unfair individual.

You may wonder if my change in attitude toward my manager altered my sorry situation. It didn't. Except that it did. You see, my situation didn't get any better, but God changed my heart, my mind, and my attitude, and those inner changes made all the difference in me. When I humbly placed myself under the submission of God and asked him for the grace to love the person who was treating me unfairly, he began to soften my heart toward that woman. Slowly, I began to see her through the eyes of Jesus. The more consistently I prayed for her, the more compassion and understanding grew within my heart.

In truth, I also learned much from her. I was young and inexperienced, and she was highly skilled and efficient. While I didn't respect her treatment of her staff, I could respect her position and her skills and abilities. By God's grace, I was able to separate the two. I honored her position and was thereby able to have a humble, gracious attitude toward her. That early lesson was foundational in my life. Through the years, there have been numerous occasions when I found myself tempted to cry foul. Thankfully, the Lord continually reminded me that he "opposes the proud but shows favor to the humble." I'd much rather be on the receiving end of God's favor than trying to go proudly alone in my own strength. Wouldn't you?

Take-away Action Thought

When I start to get angry or resentful about unfair treatment from someone, I'll go directly to this passage in 1 Peter 5 and prayerfully meditate on these powerful promises. I'll write down these verses and take them with me into the difficulty I'm facing to remind myself that God's strong and steady guidance is always with me.

My Heart's Cry to You, O Lord

Father, I feel upset about the way I'm being treated at my workplace. It's so unfair that my supervisor doesn't seem to notice or care that some of us are working hard while others are hardly working. Help me to keep coming to you with my struggles and give me the grace to leave them with you as I trust you to intervene on my behalf. Clothe me with humility, and compassion toward my offender. And please give me the wisdom I need day by day to effectively navigate this troubling situation until you remove me from it. Amen.

Practicing Grace & Gratitude

1. ***Grace & gratitude from God.*** "Humble yourselves, therefore, under God's mighty hand, that he may lift you up in due time. Cast all your anxiety on him because he cares for you." Each day this week, I'll take time to prayerfully consider anyone with whom I'm struggling or finding difficult to love. I will specifically pray for God to clothe me with humility in all situations and trust him to work on my behalf.

2. ***Grace & gratitude in me.*** "In the same way, you who are younger, submit yourselves to your elders." This week, I'll spend time praying for all those who are placed in authority over me. I'll ask God to draw them to himself if they don't have a saving faith in Jesus, and I'll pray with intentional mindfulness toward their eternal needs.

3. ***Grace & gratitude in life.*** "All of you, clothes yourselves with humility toward one another, because, 'God opposes the proud but shows favor to the humble.'" My prayer will be that God equips me to demonstrate godliness, compassion, and humility consistently wherever I am and toward whomever I'm with.

Chapter 19

An Attitude of Grace-Filled Gratitude Helps Us Persevere

But he said to me, "My grace is sufficient for you, for my power is made perfect in weakness." Therefore I will boast all the more gladly about my weaknesses, so that Christ's power may rest on me. That is why, for Christ's sake, I delight in weaknesses, in insults, in hardships, in persecutions, in difficulties. For when I am weak, then I am strong.

2 Corinthians 12:9–10

God gives us His grace in the hour we need it. If we worry about the future now, we double our pain without having the grace to deal with it.

John MacArthur

Mandy styled her ten-year-old daughter Kensie's hair into a French braid with all the attention she could muster while discreetly keeping a close watch on the clock. As the time for her daughter's oncologist's office drew nearer, she felt her insides tighten. Mandy's deft fingers had been creating visual masterpieces with Kensie's long, thick hair since she was three years old. ***She's always loved having me braid her hair***

before any special occasion, Mandy remembered. ***And today is the day we'll get the results of all those new tests. What if they indicate another round of chemo is necessary?*** The what-ifs of this most recent series of complicated tests and procedures overwhelmed her thoughts as she anxiously waited for the results that would determine their family's future for the coming months.

Gulping back the urge to cry, Mandy secured a hair tie at the bottom of Kensie's braid. "All done! Take a look in the mirror. What do you think?" Mandy asked as she passed the handheld mirror to her daughter.

Getting up and facing the bathroom mirror on the wall, Kensie studied the back of her head. "Oh Mom, it's perfect! Thank you." Then she happily announced, "I'm going to Jayne's now to wait for the other girls to arrive for the party."

"Don't forget her birthday present and card!"

Alone now, Mandy placed everything back in the drawer and gazed at her own reflection, not liking what she saw. ***I look awful. My hair's limp, I've got dark circles under my eyes, and I've lost weight. I guess the mirror is just being honest. It's a realistic picture of what I feel like on the inside. Lord, help me get through this day.***

Mechanically checking her phone again, Mandy went downstairs to the kitchen to make lunch for her husband, Jack, and herself. Absentmindedly, she gathered everything she needed on the counter and then began to rinse and chop some fruit for a side with their sandwiches. While working on lunch, she kept glancing at her phone for any messages, alerts, or missed calls. Nothing. Mandy took another deep breath and tried to calm her racing heart. She then tried thinking about what Jack says to his students in case of a fire emergency: ***Stop, drop, and roll.*** She remembered him telling a classroom full of children that if they're faced with a fire emergency, they should first stop, then drop to the floor and roll until the fire is out.

Lord, can I apply this same formula right here, right now? You know how worried I am about this newest series of test results for Kensie. I'm frightened her cancer has returned. She's only been in remission a little less than two years, and her beautiful hair is finally long enough for me to braid again. I'm scared of what I'm going to hear when the doctor's office phones today. But I need to stop worrying. I need to drop all my fears into your faithful hands. I need to roll off every what-if I'm anxious about. Help me, Lord. Please help me!

"God gives us His grace in the hour we need it," John MacArthur said in the above quote. "If we worry about the future now, we double our pain without having the grace to deal with it." The weight of this quotation grips my heart every time I stop to consider the destructive power of worry. When we worry (and we all struggle with worry), we suffer twice because Jesus tells us he gives us the grace and strength we need in the moments we require it. Not before we need it. Not after we need it. But precisely when we need it.

And who among us hasn't traveled along the same mental path as Mandy while she impatiently waited for the results of her daughter's medical tests? We've all indulged in those disastrous imaginary scenarios that quickly spiral out of control and take us to dark places in our minds. And the saddest part is that when we allow our thoughts to run away from us, we're almost always imagining our future without God in it. No matter how difficult the coming days may be, when we imagine ourselves facing a scary future without God, we've already suffered once. And without God's grace, a mighty suffering it is.

Jesus tells his followers to take note of how God provides for the birds he created, even though they don't grow and store food for themselves (Matt. 6:26). Jesus wants his brothers and sisters in the faith to take heart when called to face suffering in any shape or form and to remember that God will supply enough grace and power for us to endure.

Jesus doesn't want us to suffer twice, so how can we avoid this mental pitfall that tempts us to predict a disastrous outcome even before it occurs (if it even does!)? We ***stop*** ourselves from going down the road of unbelief that imagines our future without God in it. We ***drop*** to our knees and leave our worries, cares, and burdens with the Lord. We ***roll*** out every scary future scenario into Jesus' faithful arms, knowing that he will carry us if need be. Stop. Drop. Roll. We can do this—one thought, one worry at a time.

Take-away Action Thought

When I begin to worry about an unknown future, I will remember to stop, drop, and roll. I will implement these three grace-filled steps each and every time I need to combat my fears.

My Heart's Cry to You, O Lord

Father, today I'm facing what could be disastrous news for my loved one. I admit that I'm struggling with thoughts of worry and fear. I don't want my dear one to suffer again. My mind is full of fear-ridden memories of painful past events, and I feel overwhelmed by the thought they could happen again. Please help me to stop myself from going down this road of unbelief where I'm imagining my future without you in it. Your word tells me you will give me the grace, strength, and power I need when I need it, not before. I want to stop my habit of suffering twice because of my worry. Please help me to keep my mind on you, Jesus. Keep me in perfect peace because I trust in you. Amen.

Practicing Grace & Gratitude

1. *Grace & gratitude from God.* "My grace is sufficient for you, for my power is made perfect in weakness." When I awake in the morning, I will thank the Lord for the grace he has promised me for this day. I will face the day with a faith-infused, grace-filled expectation that no matter how it unfolds, it's under the careful administration of my heavenly Father who promises to equip me to face whatever challenges arise.
2. *Grace & gratitude in me.* "That is why, for Christ's sake, I delight in weaknesses, in insults, in hardships, in persecutions, in difficulties. For when I am weak, then I am strong." Each evening this week, I will spend a few minutes revisiting my day and reflecting on God's grace at work within me. I won't worry about my lack of strength. Rather, I'll look to God to supply me with everything I require, at every hour, to accomplish whatever he has set before me.
3. *Grace & gratitude in life.* "Therefore I will boast all the more gladly about my weaknesses, so that Christ's power may rest on me." As I consider my relationships with others, I will remind myself that everyone is in need of compassion and kindness. I won't think more highly of myself; instead, I'll pray for a humble and contrite heart, knowing that I have many glaring weaknesses of my own that, thankfully, God is still working on inside of me.

Chapter 20

An Attitude of Grace-Filled Gratitude Makes Us Holy

Rejoice in the Lord always. I will say it again: Rejoice! Let your gentleness be evident to all. The Lord is near. Do not be anxious about anything, but in every situation, by prayer and petition, with thanksgiving, present your requests to God. Finally, brothers and sisters, whatever is true, whatever is noble, whatever is right, whatever is pure, whatever is lovely, whatever is admirable—if anything is excellent or praiseworthy—think about such things.

Philippians 4:4–8

Imagine a natural seed within your heart invisibly germinating, and then extending its tender roots, branching out and growing stronger, becoming more and more entrenched until it finally fills your entire soul. That's what the seed of the gospel is like within you; it will reproduce the image of Jesus.

Elyse M. Fitzpatrick

Two mornings a week, Brenda and Cassie delivered Meals on Wheels to the house-bound elderly residents living in their rural town. It was the perfect ministry for these two close friends of many years. They had first met each other at the breakfast diner where they worked as waitresses and bonded over their shared appreciation of good food. Brenda and Cassie always made sure that what was delivered to their customers' tables was something they themselves would order, eat, and enjoy.

Once Brenda and Cassie retired, both decided they wanted to keep serving others in a similar capacity. Their only two requirements were that they hoped to minister together and that their ministry revolved around food. As Brenda looked for volunteer opportunities, she came across the idea of delivering meals to the elderly after hearing a couple from her church share how much they appreciated that daily delivery of hot, nutritious food from their local food pantry.

That's it! Brenda thought as she drove home that Sunday morning. ***Cassie will love the idea, I'm sure.*** And Cassie did. That same week, the two of them went through the interview process and within days were placed on the regular delivery schedule. A routine was quickly established where the two friends would load the van with the meals and then set out on their route. As they drove, they would pray for each recipient in turn.

At first, they didn't know anything about those on their meal delivery route other than their first and last names. But that was enough to begin interceding on behalf of their souls. Over time, Brenda and Cassie grew to intimately know each person to whom they delivered meals. In truth, these folks became like the two women's extended families.

After one especially chilly delivery day, Cassie commented on how cold she was and how good it would be to stay home the following day. When Brenda looked squarely back at her friend, they both laughed, knowing exactly what the other was thinking. "I know, I know, all right?" Cassie conceded. "The best part of our week hands-down is delivering food to those dear people, and we both know it."

Brenda agreed. "And they've blessed us more than we've blessed them! It's almost as if the tiny seed we planted in friendship with these men and women has grown into a whole garden of flowers, each one beautifully unique, each one beautiful to behold." They were both so grateful to God for giving them this perfect opportunity to share their love of a good meal to those who needed it.

What is holiness? What does it look like? The short answer is this: conformity to the image of Jesus. One of the most obvious external signs of inner holiness is how we treat others. If we're walking in step with the Spirit and keeping our thoughts on that which the Bible says is good, then our face, our hands, our feet, and our words will overflow in acts of love and words of encouragement to others.

As Brenda and Cassie discovered, by serving others with purposeful hearts and selfless deeds, they were representing Jesus to those to whom they ministered each week. Both women would tell you that they were at times tempted to become discouraged and depressed by what they saw in the homes of these elderly, often-forgotten individuals. But they didn't turn from the sadness or pain—they walked toward it and they entered in.

Isn't that what holiness looks like in the real world? It isn't just keeping oneself from evil and staying away from situations where we're tempted to sin. Holiness has hands and feet that intentionally enter into the world's pain and suffering to make a blessed difference and to tell others about the love of Jesus. And when we serve in this selfless way, others are more apt to listen because they know we truly care. When in doubt, think on Philippians 4:4–8 and watch how the seeds of holiness take root, blossom, and grow into conformity to Jesus.

Take-away Action Thought

When my thoughts begin to wander and I feel discouraged or depressed, I'll recite Philippians 4:4–8 and commit it to memory. Then I'll pray for the Lord to plant the seed of the gospel in my heart and allow it to slowly transform me into the image of Jesus.

My Heart's Cry to You, O Lord

Father, please help me be mindful of what I allow my thoughts to linger on. Help me to keep Philippians 4 at the front and center of my mind every day. I know that I'm often tempted to focus on the pain and suffering around me. I can become so sad that I grow stagnant and useless instead of trusting you to help me to make a difference. Remind me that as I keep my heart and mind on you, you are slowly changing me into the image of Jesus. Thank you for helping me to see the privilege it is to enter into others' pain and sorrow and to become your hands and feet in every situation. Amen.

Practicing Grace & Gratitude

1. *Grace & gratitude from God.* "Do not be anxious about anything, but in every situation, by prayer and petition, with thanksgiving, present your requests to God." This week, I'll stop worry in its tracks by immediately writing down in my journal anything I'm fretting about. Once I've written it out and prayed for God to handle the situation, I'll reread Philippians 4:4–8 and meditate on its truth.

2. *Grace & gratitude in me.* "And the peace of God, which transcends all understanding, will guard your hearts and your minds in Christ Jesus." This week, I'll spend time each day looking up and meditating on verses that contain the word *peace* in them. I'll also write a few out and carry them with me during the day to remind me that God says I can live in peace no matter what challenges I might face.

3. *Grace & gratitude in life.* "Finally, brothers and sisters, whatever is true, whatever is noble, whatever is right, whatever is pure, whatever is lovely, whatever is admirable—if anything is excellent or praiseworthy—think about such things." Each evening this week, I'll ask God to forgive me for any thoughts I've been indulging in that are negative, worrisome, anxious, or faithless. Then I will make a list of positive, peaceful, and faith-filled thoughts to replace them.

Chapter 21

An Attitude of Grace-Filled Gratitude Helps Us Pray

Now listen, you who say, "Today or tomorrow we will go to this or that city, spend a year there, carry on business and make money." Why, you do not even know what will happen tomorrow. What is your life? You are a mist that appears for a little while and then vanishes. Instead, you ought to say, "If it is the Lord's will, we will live and do this or that."

James 4:13–15

Anxiety won't relent, Augustine wrote, "until it finds its rest in Thee." Anxiety needs its better half in Jesus. We can be slow to get the message and spread our trust as wide as possible. But anxiety will not be quieter until it is home. We need the One who is solid and endures. And we need the One who is close and compassionate.

Edward Welch

Some months ago, a good friend told me, "I wake up every morning and realize I'm still in this nightmare." I nodded in agreement. The nightmare, without question, is the COVID-19 pandemic—and at this writing, we're still in it.

Like my friend (if not all of us), I suffer a similar dismal realization. Sometimes when I wake up, I blissfully forget about the battle we're all facing—but it doesn't take long to remember those first terrifying weeks in early 2020 of those dire mandates. The lockdowns. The closures of schools and businesses. Not seeing friends or family, especially during holidays. Not able to travel anywhere or really do much of anything. Now we're dealing with the constant mutation of the virus and new surges throughout the world. Here in the US, we've also been suffering through the sometimes-violent controversy over mask-wearing and vaccines, while illness and death continues to hit more of our loved ones. At this writing (early 2022), the US has climbed to over 900,000 people who have died from the virus. As the winter turns to spring, we all have the hope to return to some normalcy soon.

Who wouldn't consider this ongoing scenario nightmarish? Our entire world has been upended by something so small it's not visible to the human eye, and yet so powerful it's taken entire nations captive. It doesn't matter if you're pro-vaccine, anti-vaccine, or just not this particular vaccine—each of us continues to fight a very personal battle with not only this virus but our ever-changing, increasingly volatile world.

With a spouse who teaches in a public school and a daughter who is a social worker in several schools, I'm not surprised when they share how these last two years have shaken everyone, from faculty and staff to the students and their families. There's certainly no shortage of fear, unrest, and unease about the worldwide uncertainties we face. This is why today is the day to surrender our lives into the care and keeping of our Lord and Savior Jesus Christ. The only One, as Welch states, "who is solid and endures . . . the One who is close and compassionate."

Morning by morning, I've been trying to break the dismal habit of silently groaning, "Oh, no, I'm still living in this nightmare," by engaging instead in a more God-honoring wake-up prayer: "Thank you, Lord, for this day. I will rejoice and be glad in it. With your abiding strength, I will walk through this day with a grace-filled heart of gratitude, and I will submit my will to yours in every area. Amen." This has become my new morning prayer, and ever so slowly I'm discovering that my heart attitude and my emotions are falling in line with a greater truth: God is in charge. I am not. And I can rest in that comforting truth, even when I don't know what tomorrow will bring.

Learning to rest in God when anxiety about the unknowns of today and tomorrow threatens to undo us can be one of the most valuable spiritual lessons we learn in this life. It is also one of the most difficult. For some reason, we try in vain to control our circumstances in order to minimize our pain or avoid suffering at all costs. This is completely understandable given the pain and suffering so common in our broken world! But it is also why most of us have probably spent an overabundance of time and energy attempting to figure out how to avoid the serious effects of COVID and the devastating aftermath affecting us socially, economically, and even spiritually.

Learning to rest in God during a worldwide pandemic that has ushered in formerly unknown restrictions and loss of personal freedoms is possible. In chapter 4 of his letter, James explains how we need to approach our pain, suffering, and uncertainty: by coming to God in prayer with an attitude of grace-filled gratitude for his personal presence and provision for us. When we realize that we are, as James aptly describes, "a mist," we can then draw near to God in prayer as he draws near to us. We can't say it too many times: "We need the One who is solid and endures. And we need the One who is close and compassionate." Thank him today for being solid, enduring, close, and compassionate.

Take-away Action Thought

During those moments when I feel like I'm living in a real-life nightmare, I will stop myself from mentally revisiting the difficulties of these past months or even years. Instead, I will take my thoughts captive in Christ and start thanking God for his rock-solid love for me. I'll praise him for being the One who endures for all time and who sovereignly rules even now. Then I'll give him thanks for being my righteous and faithful heavenly Father who comes close and showers me with compassion every morning.

My Heart's Cry to You, O Lord

Father, I ask that you help me to stop waking up every morning with feelings of dread and discouragement. It's true that these past long months have been frightening and uncommonly difficult. Our lives have changed in ways we could not have imagined. Please give me your grace and strength to live one day at a time and to not worry about tomorrow. Shower me with your divine wisdom and show me how to live fully present today. Bestow on me your compassions, which are new every morning, and teach me how giving thanks with a heart of gratitude will powerfully transform my thoughts and my emotions. I thank you for the perfect peace only you can supply. Amen.

Practicing Grace & Gratitude

1. *Grace & gratitude from God.* "You ought to say, 'If it is the Lord's will, we will live and do this or that.'" Beginning today, I will be mindful of closing every prayer by asking for God's will in all circumstances. I want to focus on the biblical truth that no matter what I desire or pray for, God's will in all matters is truly best for me.
2. *Grace & gratitude in me.* "What is your life? You are a mist that appears for a little while and then vanishes." This week, I'll spend time asking the Lord to help me reframe my prayers so that they overflow with grace-filled words and an attitude of gratefulness. My prayers should reflect my belief that God is sovereign, while I am here only a short while, with limited understanding of his perfect plan.
3. *Grace & gratitude in life.* "Why, you do not even know what will happen tomorrow." Each evening this week, I will spend some time praying with a grateful heart. I will use this time to give thanks for every blessing, every mercy, and every show of compassion from the Lord I can recall. Then I'll end my prayer by acknowledging to God that I understand how limited my knowledge is of what he is accomplishing through world events that often trouble me so greatly.

Chapter 22

Learning How to Pray with Grace & Gratitude

"This, then, is how you should pray:

"'Our Father in heaven,
hallowed be your name,
your kingdom come,
your will be done,
    on earth as it is in heaven.
Give us today our daily bread.
And forgive us our debts,
    as we also have forgiven our debtors.
And lead us not into temptation,
    but deliver us from the evil one.'"

Matthew 6:9–13

How beautiful is the sweet glow of mercy on the face of Jesus. How special are the arms held open wide to welcome me to his side. How piercing are his eyes, penetrating me with his love and understanding. The mouth of Jesus shares both laughter and smiles of contentment. His words beckon me.

Kathy Carlton Willis

Jenny was the only biological child of her parents, Eleanor and Ethan. However, from as early on as she could remember, her home was full of foster children rotating in and out as the need arose. A young Jenny never knew how to answer those who asked her how many brothers and sisters she had. She couldn't answer because that number was always changing. From middle-of-the-night emergency placements to the calmly scheduled middle-of-the-day arrivals, Jenny's home life was never the same for very long.

Since she knew nothing different, this shifting family dynamic was normal to her. In fact, Jenny believed she had a better home life than other kids because of how her parents chose to handle foster parenting. Rather than become impatient or frustrated with a particularly difficult child, who was clearly hurting and acting out, Jenny's parents found creative ways to maintain order while demonstrating unconditional love to each child. One thing was true about Jenny's home life: it was never boring!

Her parents' lifelong commitment to creating a home where anyone was welcome was not lost on Jenny. She often considered it a matter of course that when she grew up and married, she would follow in her mom and dad's footsteps and become a foster parent herself. By her late twenties, Jenny had not yet married, but her strong desire to become a foster mom led her to begin the application and training process anyway. Despite living alone, Jenny prayed long and hard about this life-changing decision. ***Only God knows when I will get married***, Jenny told herself. ***But until then, I have the means and the ability to offer a safe space to a hurting child. And I have plenty of experience***! "Lord," she prayed aloud one day, "Please either open this door wide or close it tightly shut. You know my heart's desire. If it's your will for me to foster as a single woman, then let it come to pass. Amen."

Jenny learned many important life lessons from her God-honoring, servant-minded parents. She often unconsciously mimicked their selfless and diligent work ethic. Jenny never even considered the possibility that she wouldn't follow in their footsteps. But as a young single woman, she recognized that when her mom and dad faced challenges her parents faced as foster dad and mom, they dealt with them together. If she decided to become a foster mom alone, then Jenny knew it would be difficult.

So she prayed. She longed to share the goodness and love of Jesus with children who had seen nothing in their young lives but suffering and hardship. She prayed that God might use her as an instrument of healing and hope in their tender lives. Jenny was ready to enter into the foster parent program with her eyes wide open; and because she knew what she was getting herself into, she prayed all the more.

Jenny wisely made it a daily practice to spend time with the Lord, praying from a place of both grace and gratitude. She thanked the Lord for her blessed upbringing and the example her parents set before her. She asked him to prepare her for the possibility of fostering children who might come to her troubled and in trouble, knowing she would need his sustaining strength every day.

Like Jenny, each of us has been fitted for service by the Almighty. Even if our parents weren't the ones who modeled such selfless servanthood, we can all learn from others who do take the lead in selfless service. As Jenny understood, each of us needs to come before our heavenly Father in prayer and ask him to open and shut the doors as he wills. For we must also understand that none of us can serve in an effective way without God as our partner, our guide, and our merciful sustainer.

Take-away Action Thought

Before I enter into a new area of service or ministry, I'll spend time praying for God's wisdom and will to be accomplished in and through me. I won't run ahead of his plan, his timing, or his will for me. Instead, I'll wait patiently for him to make the way apparent to me.

My Heart's Cry to You, O Lord

Father, my heart is bursting to start serving in this new capacity. I'm so excited, and I have so many new ideas to put into practice. Help me to rein in my enthusiasm and learn to wait patiently on you. In my heart of hearts, I know I can't accomplish anything, large or small, without you. Please bestow on me your wisdom and divine understanding. Give me the insight I need to proceed if this is your will. Thank you for your grace, which enables me to rest securely in an unknown future. Amen.

Practicing Grace & Gratitude

1. *Grace & gratitude from God.* "Our Father in heaven, hallowed be your name, your kingdom come, your will be done, on earth as it is in heaven." Each morning this week, I'll spend a few minutes in prayer asking for the Lord's will to be accomplished in my life and throughout the world. Then I'll give thanks, confident that God's

perfect plan will come to pass because he is sovereign over heaven and earth.

2. *Grace & gratitude in me.* "Lead us not into temptation, but deliver us from the evil one." Every afternoon, I will ask the Lord for wisdom and grace to know what his perfect will is for me in all matters. If I begin to feel impatient and am tempted to run ahead of God when I'm not sure of his will in a specific matter, I'll stop, confess my impatience, and learn to wait, by trusting in his timing and plan for me.

3. *Grace & gratitude in life.* "Give us today our daily bread." Before bedtime this week, I'll prayerfully recount the many tangible and intangible blessings of that day. I'll give thanks for each one, knowing that God loves to give to me blessings he uniquely tailors for me.

Chapter 23

Changing the World by Witnessing with Grace & Gratitude

The earth is the LORD's, and everything in it,
the world, and all who live in it;
for he founded it on the seas
and established it on the waters.
Who may ascend the mountain of the LORD?
Who may stand in his holy place?
The one who has clean hands and a pure heart,
who does not trust in an idol
or swear by a false god.
They will receive blessing from the LORD
and vindication from God their Savior.

Psalm 24:1–5

Christ is our Redeemer, Deliverer, Reconciler, Mediator, Intercessor, Advocate, Attorney, Solicitor, our Hope, Comfort, Shield, Protection, Defender, Strength, Health, Satisfaction and Salvation.

William Tyndale

Five years ago, Cary lost her adult son to sudden heart failure. Jacob had been driving his truck home from work when he veered off the highway. By the time the rescue team arrived on the scene, it was too late. Cary still remembers the late-night phone call that changed her world forever. It took her months to process the truth that her son wasn't coming back. It was at least two years before she was able to get up in the morning without her first thoughts being of Jacob and how he died. Grief stalked Cary for a long, long time.

But eventually, her grief transformed into something very different. During the first weeks after Jacob's death, she was numb. Beyond tears, she walked through her days like a robot and functioned on automatic for months. Then, slowly, her emotions began to reawaken, and she began to heal. As time went on, Cary clung to the Lord and frequently recited Psalm 24 back to the Lord as she prayed: "The earth is the Lord's, and everything in it, the world, and all who live in it."

As she humbly acknowledged God's ownership and sovereignty over all of life, Cary started to see the world as a fragile place to live in a way she had not done so before. Life was tenuous and unpredictable, and she realized that truth more than most. As God continued to mend her broken heart, she discovered a renewed desire to begin living again. After praying about next steps, Cary felt compelled to bring the gospel into every encounter she had with another person. And she did. Now, she tells her story to anyone who will listen.

Because of her life-altering loss, Cary found she had a ready audience with whomever she conversed. She hardly even needed an invitation to tell others the good news of Jesus Christ and how God had met her in her darkest hours. Cary didn't wait for official speaking requests at her church or formal gatherings with small groups of fellow believers to tell her story. She made use of ordinary days and settings to share the extraordinary way

God had worked on her behalf. She knew firsthand that he is the giver of life, the sustainer of life, and the blessed redeemer of our lives. And she made it her mission to share that good news with everyone she met.

Whether we're experiencing a season where ordinary life and days comprise the majority of our time or are mired in a catastrophic, life-altering difficulty, we can find present help, present hope, and present grace to see us through. While Cary's passion to share the good news to everyone was ignited by her loss and pain, we don't have to wait. We can take on the same mantle of urgency right now and begin witnessing with grace and gratitude what God has done in our lives.

Life is fragile and uncertain. We all recognize these difficult realities. Sadly, most of us don't possess the internal drive to share our faith with others until we've faced circumstances that pierce our hearts and souls. But why wait? Why not speak up and speak out to those who may be ready hearers of the good news today? When we study the Bible and have a correct understanding of God's ownership and sovereignty over all of life, we see that while we can rest in our saving faith in Jesus, others can't if they're not told.

As Cary discovered on the path to healing and restoration after the death of her son, we can immediately begin telling others about Jesus in every ordinary situation, on every ordinary day. And when we do tell others about our Savior with grace and gratitude, there will be nothing ordinary about it!

Take-away Action Thought

When I lose sight of what is most urgent in life—sharing my faith with others and telling them what God has done for me—I'll pause and reflect on the fragility and uncertainty of life on earth. Then I'll remind myself that the Holy Spirit will give me the words to speak as one of God's witnesses if only I'm willing.

My Heart's Cry to You, O Lord

Father, I don't want to wait to realize how fragile and uncertain life is. I already have evidence of your presence and provision in my life that I can share with others who still need you. Please help me to be an eager and faithful witness for you. Give me the right words to speak so that others can know of your glory and goodness. May I use every opportunity to share with grace and gratitude about your forgiveness and love for all people. Amen.

Practicing Grace & Gratitude

1. *Grace & gratitude from God.* "They will receive blessing from the Lord and vindication from God their Savior." Each day this week, I'll be intentional about witnessing what God has done for me, and I'll share the good news of Jesus Christ as I'm able.

2. *Grace & gratitude in me.* "Who may ascend the mountain of the Lord? Who may stand in his holy place? The one who has clean hands and a pure heart, who does

not trust in an idol or swear by a false god." During my quiet moments with God, I'll prayerfully reflect on how lacking I've been in seeing the urgency of sharing the gospel with others. I'll pray for God to continue to open doors to me to speak and for him to give me the courage to open my mouth when these opportunities arise.

3. *Grace & gratitude in life.* "The earth is the Lord's, and everything in it, the world, and all who live in it; for he founded it on the seas and established it on the waters." As I start intentionally witnessing to others, I'll also pray for them, recognizing that God is the giver of new life and that I'm privileged to speak for him.

Chapter 24

Grace-Filled Gratitude Changes How We View Our Weaknesses

You created my inmost being;
    you knit me together in my mother's womb.
I praise you because I am fearfully and wonderfully made;
    your works are wonderful,
    I know that full well.
My frame was not hidden from you
    when I was made in the secret place,
    when I was woven together in the depths of the earth.

Psalm 139:13–15

When I understand that everything happening to me is to make me more Christ like, it resolves a great deal of anxiety.

A. W. Tozer

Kinsey stared at the wall in the examination room as she waited for her cardiologist to arrive. She wondered how her sister Brielle was faring in her final volleyball game of the season. Not that Kinsey would know what it felt like to be part of any of Brielle's competitive sports teams. For as long as she could remember, she had been the onlooker to all of Brielle's games. Born with a congenital heart defect, she had never been able to participate in any of her sister's rigorous sports activities. *Always the observer, that's what I am*, thought Kinsey.

As she waited patiently for her doctor, she considered how different her life was compared to Brielle's—and to most of her friends too. It wasn't as though Kinsey envied their ability to participate in their high school sporting events, but sometimes she had to admit it was hard to watch her peers plan for weekend runs and challenging hikes in the mountains. Kinsey accepted that her heart couldn't take the strain of these physically demanding activities, but she sometimes worried about what her future would look like after she graduated and went on to college.

Will I be able to do all the normal things other college students do? Am I strong enough to live on my own in a dorm room? Will Dad and Mom even let me move into a dorm? That's the bigger question. Kinsey knew she wanted to try. And today her cardiologist would help them decide whether or not it was a possibility. *If I'm careful to follow all of his guidelines*, Kinsey thought, *then maybe going away to college will be a real option for me.*

She reached into her backpack and removed her college folder. While she waited, she would start making two lists for the fall: cans and cannots. *Let's start planning how to make the transition from home to college life possible. I know it might be a hard sell, but Dad and Mom are reasonable. They just want me to understand the risks involved in moving out of their home and into one of my own.* Kinsey prayed out loud: "Help me, Lord, to know my limitations and not endanger myself by being reckless. You already know my strengths and weaknesses because you created me. I know you have a plan for my life, and that's all I need to know."

When we embrace a biblically accurate view of God as our Creator, our Savior, and our Sustainer, accepting our weaknesses and inabilities is much easier. This understanding of God's sovereignty means we understand that any limitations or struggles we encounter are part of God's perfect design and plan for us. Knowing that we have been his from the beginning of time should make us content and confident in how his love toward us is expressed, even when this love looks different for us than it does for others around us.

Because we understand that God wants only what is best for us and that he frequently uses our natural weaknesses as the driving components to transform us into the image of Jesus, we can rest in this precious truth. As we learn to accept weaknesses within ourselves as divine blessings that continually propel us into the arms of Christ, what once appeared as detriments transform into conduits of God's amazing grace. The apostle Paul learned this very truth when he wrote 2 Corinthians 12:8–9:

> Three times I pleaded with the Lord to take it away from me. But he said to me, "My grace is sufficient for you, for my power is made perfect in weakness." Therefore I will boast all the more gladly about my weaknesses, so that Christ's power may rest on me.

Paul learned that the weakness he experienced was part of God's plan for him to continually rely on God's grace. Like Paul, we too can learn to accept our weaknesses, thank God for them, and give thanks for the grace God promises us in each and every situation.

Take-away Action Thought

When I feel discouraged or anxious about my weaknesses and limitations, I will read Psalm 139 and remember that God knew me and planned every detail of my being before time. I will thank him for the grace he supplies that overcomes all my weaknesses and is sufficient for my every need.

My Heart's Cry to You, O Lord

Father, help me to accept my weaknesses as part of your perfect plan for my life. Give me the wisdom and understanding to fully grasp that you are my Creator, my Savior, and my Sustainer. Help me to recognize that despite my weaknesses, your grace is sufficient to supply all my needs. I want to honor you by trusting you, even when I face challenges others may not. Let my faith in your perfect plan be evident to all who know me. As a child of the Most High, I can experience perfect peace because I know that you are in control of all that concerns me. Amen.

Practicing Grace & Gratitude

1. *Grace & gratitude from God.* "For you created my inmost being; you knit me together in my mother's womb." Each day this week, I'll read Psalm 139 and highlight the verses that stand out to me. I'll read these verses with the understanding that God is my Creator, Savior, and Sustainer.

2. *Grace & gratitude in me.* "I praise you because I am fearfully and wonderfully made; your works are wonderful, I know that full well." This week, I'll talk with God about my weaknesses and how they have impacted my life. I'll be honest about any frustrations or disappointments I've experienced because of these limitations, but I won't stop there. Instead, I'll close out my time with the Lord by thanking him for these divine opportunities to see his grace meet my every need.
3. *Grace & gratitude in life.* "My frame was not hidden from you when I was made in the secret place, when I was woven together in the depths of the earth." Each morning, I will give thanks to God for his all-sufficient grace. I'll intentionally look for evidence of his perfect provision tailored exactly for me as I go through my day.

Chapter 25

Grace-Filled Gratitude Changes How We Think

For the word of God is alive and active. Sharper than any double-edged sword, it penetrates even to dividing soul and spirit, joints and marrow; it judges the thoughts and attitudes of the heart. Nothing in all creation is hidden from God's sight. Everything is uncovered and laid bare before the eyes of him to whom we must give account.

Hebrews 4:12–13

Why do we seldom go through a day without some experience of conflict? The answer is that we think of our lives as our own, and we are more committed to the purposes of our own kingdom than we are to God's. We need to recognize that the people in our way have been sent to us by a wise and sovereign King. He never gets a wrong address and always chooses just the right moment to expose our hearts and realign them to his.

Paul David Tripp

Dena impatiently drummed her fingers on the steering wheel of her SUV. *Hurry up, boys or we're going to be late again! Why don't they listen to me when I tell them anything?* Scanning the school building from end to end, she finally spotted Derek, sporting his neon orange backpack. "There's one, now where's the other?" she said aloud. Honking the horn, she kept her eyes steeled on her oldest son's movements, waiting for him to respond to her audible summons. But Derek was having too much fun with his friends to take any notice of his mom's incessant horn tapping.

Finally, having had enough, Dena removed her keys from the ignition, got out of the car, and stomped over to where her son was happily chatting with his friends, oblivious to her attempts to get his attention. "Excuse me, Derek," she said with a firmness normally reserved for inside their home. "We have to go. Now. Where is your brother?" Derek shrugged at his mom and then went right back to talking with his schoolmates.

A little more insistent this time, Dena raised her voice a few notches and pulled her son around to face her.

"*What*?" Derek demanded.

"In the car. Now." Dena's frustration punctuated every syllable.

Derek knew that look and recognized his mother's tone. "See you guys later," he called over his shoulder.

At the car, Dena said with quiet fury in her voice, "I told you both we had to leave immediately after school today. Didn't you remember? And where's Elliot?"

"Mom, I don't know. Should I go back and see if I can find him?"

"Yes and make it fast."

Derek tore across the lawn and was back inside the school before Dena could start on another rant. Dena felt her heart pound and was sure her blood pressure must be rising too.

Why does this happen every time we need to be somewhere? Dena prayed. *Why don't my boys listen to me? I'm so tired of trying to get them to obey. Days like these make me hate parenting.*

They also make me despise myself when I get so angry. Help me, Lord! I'm feeling so derailed by the struggles in parenting that I've lost sight of the tremendous gift being a parent is. Please forgive me for giving in to complaining when I should be focusing on all that you have blessed me with. And my sons are at the top of that wonderful list!

Dena, like most moms (and dads), was feeling the double-edged sword of parenting from a fallible, human perspective, and it was taking her down a self-defeating path. She loved her boys and tried to parent them in God-honoring ways, but she neglected to notice that while her boys needed to learn to honor and obey her instructions, she had a heart that also required adjustment. Ouch. Her own lack of gratitude in the attitude department was making her parenting difficulties even harder.

Before Dena had gotten married and had her sons, she had created in her mind what her perfect imaginary family would look like: how her children would behave and, specifically, how she would successfully parent them. What she hadn't considered was that although we all desire to have life work out as we've imagined, it often doesn't—and then we have our own hearts to reckon with. Dena also had neglected the power of honing a heart of gratitude even in the midst of parenting messiness and inevitable relational conflicts.

Paul Tripp's statement about how seldom any of us experience a whole day without some kind of conflict is so true! This type of conflict reveals the idols within our hearts. Take Dena, for example. She has a good desire for her children to be respectful and obedient. But underneath this seemingly appropriate desire is something Dena desires even more: she wants a peaceful day.

She doesn't want to have to instruct and guide and sometimes discipline her boys. She wants them to behave in the way she expects, and when they don't, Dena gets angry.

This is exactly the sort of situation where Hebrews 4 can redirect her heart and mind back toward biblical truth, where she can do some soul searching about why she feels so upset and conflicted about her parenting. As Dena learns to open her own heart and her motives before the Lord, she will better understand her own angst about her sons and recognize that perhaps she has been thinking unbiblically about interruptions in own life. Consider Tripp's words: "We need to recognize that the people in our way have been sent to us by a wise and sovereign King. He never gets a wrong address and always chooses just the right moment to expose our hearts and realign them to his." Each of us needs to have our hearts exposed before our heavenly Father, who can realign them to his own heart. And developing a heart that defaults to grace-driven gratitude is a beautiful place to begin.

Take-away Action Thought

When the struggles and conflicts of the day start to irritate me, I'll step back from the situation and take a few moments to ask the Lord to help me see these trials as divinely orchestrated interruptions. I'll reread Hebrews 4:12–13 and commit these verses to memory as a reminder that how I think about conflict is important.

My Heart's Cry to You, O Lord

Father, today was another real trial for me. I was having such a wonderful morning and then suddenly everything fell apart. Things went wrong. My family stopped listening. We were late to our appointments, and I wanted to give up on them and on myself! I'm so tired of this fighting and conflict. Please teach me how to navigate these challenges in a way that honors you. Help me to look inside my own heart and mind; reveal to me any areas where I am erecting idols to myself. I don't want to live life to please myself. I want you to always be on the throne of my heart, enabling me to love, serve, and sacrifice for those in my life. And I know that as I seek to develop a heart that is full of gratitude, I will be much more able to work through these inevitable relational challenges. Amen.

Practicing Grace & Gratitude

1. *Grace & gratitude from God.* "For the word of God is alive and active." Each day this week, I'll spend time thanking God for how he uses his powerful word to work new life into my heart and mind. I'll spend time reflecting on how different portions of Scripture provide me with exactly what I need on any given day.

2. *Grace & gratitude in me.* "Everything is uncovered and laid bare before the eyes of him to whom we must give account." In prayer this week, I'll ask the Lord to reveal to me any idols I have built in my heart. I'll confess these sinful desires and ask God to help me to think biblically about the challenges, interruptions, or conflicts that come into my life.

3. *Grace & gratitude in life.* "Sharper than any double-edged sword, it penetrates even to dividing soul and spirit, joints and marrow; it judges the thoughts and attitudes of the heart." This week, I'll pray specifically for my family to search and understand the true thoughts and motives of their hearts. I'll ask the Lord to show us all whether we're gladly, gratefully, and willingly submitting to his plans for us or resisting him because we desire our own will more.

Chapter 26

Grace-Filled Gratitude Changes How We Speak

The Lord has done it this very day;
let us rejoice today and be glad. . . .
You are my God, and I will praise you;
you are my God, and I will exalt you.

Psalm 118:24, 28

Over the years, I've learned not simply to think less of myself but to think about myself less. When I'm thinking most about Jesus, I'm most happy.

Randy Alcorn

In the space of five short months, a close friend of mine had to choose how to react to the bittersweet news that two of her adult sons, their wives, and twelve of her grandchildren were moving states away. During that time of transition, both sons and their families lived with my friend and her husband. She recalls it being wonderful and heartbreaking all at the same time.

It would have been so easy to give in to sadness and grief with both sons moving so far away. But my friend took a different path as she worked through her motherly emotions. Instead of getting up each morning and checking off one day closer to their move date, she decided to invest herself, her love, and her words in the short time they still had together.

My friend got on her smartphone and downloaded a Bible study app. She took the time to search out studies that would be of interest to her grandchildren, near and far. After selecting age-appropriate studies, she invited each of her grandchildren to join her. They could work through the lessons and share their comments, questions, or concerns.

Amazingly, most of her grandchildren opted in! She was absolutely delighted. Together, they would read a passage of Scripture, go through the comments and supportive materials, and then answer the questions. What was truly thrilling was how each grandchild jumpstarted the conversation by sharing their own specific questions and thoughts about the text.

Each biblical principle shared among them was also discussed and prayed over. My friend told me how blessed she was to have taken part in these Bible studies with her precious grandkids. And now that they have established this together, they can continue to participate in more studies together—whether they live nearby or hundreds of miles away.

My friend wisely recognized that her sons' move was going to deeply affect them all. She knew emotions would be running high, so she decided to be proactive with her inner heart attitude by speaking forth grace-filled words of gratitude about all the good God was doing in their lives. And her intentionality about thinking less about herself and more about Jesus was contagious. Her family testifies to the power of a thankful heart that praises God for his perfect day-to-day provision.

How we choose to respond to life's unexpected, unwanted, and perhaps even heartbreaking situations speaks volumes. We make an intentional choice each time we speak about something, good or bad. And our words have power. As my friend discovered early on, if she had allowed herself to wallow in sadness and become paralyzed by her sorrow, she would have missed the opportunity to make an eternal impact.

Words demonstrate what we believe, what we think, and how we feel. Our words either deflate our listeners or encourage their hearts. Our words either build their faith or they breed doubt. Our words will either magnify our Lord or cause others to blame him. So learning to speak truth, to give praise, to offer thanks, and to rejoice in all that God has done and is doing matters!

My friend also understood another key element to using her words wisely. She learned to think of herself less often and think more about Jesus. The wonderful result? Happiness from deep within began to permeate her heart and soul. Yes, even in the midst of personal sorrow, we can choose our words wisely and thereby watch how our attitudes and emotions follow. Words matter.

Take-away Action Thought

When I'm tempted to despair over an unwanted change or difficult news, I won't complain. Instead, I'll make praising God and rejoicing in what he is doing my default response. I'll choose to glorify God with my words because words are powerful, and they matter.

My Heart's Cry to You, O Lord

Father, I want to give thanks to you today for the wonderful way you orchestrate blessings all around me. I admit I've been tempted to complain when life hands me unwanted change or difficult news. But I know that as I turn toward you and ask for your divine wisdom to permeate my heart and mind, you begin to show me the beauty even in the pain. Help me to honor you by trusting you. Help me to use my words to praise you, to rejoice in you, and to encourage others to put the full weight of their care and concerns into your faithful hands. Thank you for your patience with me when I struggle to magnify you with my words. Amen.

Practicing Grace & Gratitude

1. *Grace & gratitude from God.* "The Lord has done it this very day; let us rejoice today and be glad." This week, I'll be intentional about listening to praise and worship music whenever I am able. I'll play these God-exalting songs and hymns at home, in my car, and whenever I'm alone.
2. *Grace & gratitude in me.* "You are my God, and I will praise you." This week, I'll spend time writing down what I'm thankful for in my journal under headings such as "family," "friends," "church," "work," "health," "finances." I'll then be intentional about noticing the goodness of God in every area of my life.
3. *Grace & gratitude in life.* "You are my God, and I will exalt you." When I spend time with the Lord each day, I'll focus most on exalting him and giving thanks to him rather than in simply submitting requests. Then I'll take note of how this shift in prayer has changed my attitude toward the challenges I'm facing.

Chapter 27

Grace-Filled Gratitude Changes How We Live

Trust in the LORD with all your heart
and lean not on your own understanding;
in all your ways submit to him,
and he will make your paths straight.

Proverbs 3:5–6

I find my own perspective changes when I can let the present be something God is shaping for a future I cannot see—and that something is good because God is good. Even in the darker moments when I wonder if I have indeed missed God through my own hardheadedness (a genuine possibility), I am comforted by remembering that I belong to Christ—and I cannot, then, be truly lost again. It helps me to stop looking so hard for the certain and lean the weight of my life on the God who owns them all.

Paula Rinehart

Grace's hands trembled as she clicked "send" on her resignation letter. Although she had worked at that elementary school for over thirty years, she knew it was time to move on. It was time to let go of her treasured career so she could spend more time with other children—her beloved grandchildren.

At the beginning of every new year, Grace and her husband Steve conducted an annual planning meeting. Once the holidays were a thing of the past, all the decorations stored away, and celebrations behind them, Grace and Steve would gather their planning tools: their current and projected finances, their healthcare plans, and their dreams and desires for life after retirement.

Hands down, the number one priority was for both of them to have the opportunities to spend more time with their eight grandchildren. Of their three adult children, only one lived nearby. The other two lived at opposite ends of the country, which meant that each year they saw two of their children and grandchildren only once during the holidays and once during the summer months. It just wasn't enough anymore. Grace especially felt the desire to invest more of herself into her quickly growing grandchildren because at work, she was reminded daily of the needs all children have, and she longed to shower love on her own grandkids.

When her third-grade class celebrated Grandparents' Day, Grace felt real regret that she wasn't able to be with her own grandchildren at their schools so far away. When she decorated her classroom for each of the holidays, she often felt sad for the same reason. So at long last, she and Steve mutually decided that this would be her final year to teach.

As soon as this decision was made, however, Grace began to experience doubt and fear. What would her life look like if she wasn't teaching? She realized that much of her identity was defined by her role as a teacher. It was a bit overwhelming to think about. Still, Grace believed it was time for her to take a leap of faith and begin something new. So she did.

Change can be unsettling and daunting—even frightening! Especially when we've invested long and hard in a career, a home, a church, or a relationship. And yet, there is a time for change in each of our lives. As Grace and Steve realized, even with all their wise planning, the conclusion of one life season to make way for the next can be daunting. Both of them quickly recognized they would need to learn how to remake their lives as a retired couple. They would now have more time at their disposal. They would have to learn how to spend these hours and days in their new life—one that was still fruitful for the Lord.

Grace felt her heartstrings tug at her whenever she thought about permanently giving up teaching, until Steve pointed out to her, "Honey, you'll always be a teacher. It's in your blood. Now you'll just be using all that creativity and skills to teach our grandchildren."

She nodded and said, "But it's still hard."

Steve grabbed her hand, and together they gave thanks for their long and fruitful careers and how God had blessed their efforts all along the way.

As they continued to make their plans for the coming months and years, a slow and steady peace enveloped them both. The more they talked to each other about upcoming visits with their children and grandchildren, the more they felt their excitement grow. More importantly, they intentionally spent more time before the Lord, asking him to direct their paths wherever they may lead.

Take-away Action Thought

When I'm about to embark on a new life venture, I'll be intentional about spending quality time with God each and every day. I'll meditate on Proverbs 3 that assures me that as I trust in the Lord and submit to him, he will make my paths straight.

My Heart's Cry to You, O Lord

Father, please help me to trust you with this change in my life. Although I believe that you have led me to choose this new path, I still feel uncertain at times. It's hard to let go of all that's so familiar to me. I want to feel peace and confidence in your guidance as I step out in faith, but I'm often nervous and I sometimes waver. Give me your divine wisdom and understanding and make my paths straight. Help me to enter into this new season of life, this fresh new opportunity to serve others in love, with a grace-filled heart of gratitude. Amen.

Practicing Grace & Gratitude

1. *Grace & gratitude from God.* "Trust in the LORD with all your heart and lean not on your own understanding." Every morning this week, I'll begin my day with a prayer of thanks to God for caring for me, providing for me, and making a way for me according to his perfect, eternal plan.

2. ***Grace & gratitude in me.*** "In all your ways submit to him." At mealtimes this week, along with giving thanks for the food set before me, I'll thank the Lord for protecting me from harm and for orchestrating my paths through life even when I don't always understand where the next step might take me.
3. ***Grace & gratitude in life.*** "He will make your paths straight." At the close of each day, I'll prayerfully reflect on my day and be especially mindful of how God walked ahead of me wherever I stepped. I will sleep in peace, knowing that God watches over me day and night.

Chapter 28

Grace-Filled Gratitude Changes How We Prioritize Our Time

You, my brothers and sisters, were called to be free. But do not use your freedom to indulge the flesh; rather, serve one another humbly in love. For the entire law is fulfilled in keeping this one command: "Love your neighbor as yourself."

Galatians 5:13–14

Resolved, never to do anything which I would be afraid to do if it were the last hour of my life.

Jonathan Edwards

Kelsey was a flight attendant whose work sometimes took her out of town for several weeks. As a single woman, she relied heavily on her family and a few close friends to keep her current with whatever was happening in their hometown. They also made it a point to spend as much time as they could with her when she was home. While Kelsey loved her job, she was starting to feel the pull to transition into a position that would allow her to work at the airport near her home.

She had spent ten years as a flight attendant and had traveled much of the world during that time. Kelsey made the most of her weekend layovers in the major cities across the ocean and had explored historical sites most people she knew only dreamed about visiting. So what was the drawback? The longer she stayed in this career, the more she felt herself beginning to lose her youthful wanderlust. She now longed for more routine and stability in her life. Though she got along wonderfully with her colleagues, Kelsey often felt the pressure to join her coworkers in off-duty activities that were certainly not honoring to God. Politely, she would beg off and therefore found herself alone most of the time. For Kelsey, a real people person, this lack of genuine fellowship was painful, and she increasingly felt the sting of loneliness.

That isolation, along with the fact that whenever she was home, she spent much of her time playing catch-up with her family and friends, made her even more eager for a change. The final straw broke when Kelsey's sister Cora gave birth to her first child, and Kelsey could only celebrate through a brief phone conversation. When her heartstrings tugged more than ever, she decided to make the dream of a career change a reality.

Today, Kelsey works in town and is able to spend her time off investing in her family and friends like never before. The stuff of ordinary life feels extraordinary to her because God has opened up a whole vista of service opportunities for her. No longer does Kelsey have to decline invitations for socializing and serving. She can say yes! Although Kelsey lived the dream many fantasize about, she discovered that no matter where you travel, there truly is no place like home.

No matter where we wander, having a settled space to call our own is priceless. As Kelsey happily discovered once she made the huge transition from traveling to working locally, having a permanent home meant she no longer felt like an outsider trying to work her way back into her family's and friends' lives. Kelsey also realized how much she valued her relationships. It deeply pained her to continually say goodbye, often just when she was just getting reacquainted and involved at home.

Not everyone will feel the need to make the major life transition Kelsey did, but the reasons behind her decision are worth pondering. She longed for deep spiritual connections with her family and friends. She longed to "do life" on a daily basis with these dear folks, and she knew it was impossible until she made a move home. So home she came. Kelsey was immensely grateful for her tenure as a flight attendant. But the more she saw of the world, beautiful though it was, her heart drew her back to ministry and service in a deeper way.

Kelsey also discovered that her own spiritual life blossomed and grew once she stayed home. She was finally able to fellowship with her church family every week, thereby cementing their spiritual bond. For Kelsey, and for each of us, it's all about prioritizing what matters most in life. Given the brief time each of us has on earth, it would do us well to spend some time prayerfully looking at where, what, why, and how we invest one of our most precious commodities: our time. May we spend it in that which will endure for all eternity.

Take-away Action Thought

When I get distracted by the world and what it can offer, I'll remember that my time on earth is short and that I want to spend my hours and days investing in that which lasts for all eternity. What does the Bible say lasts forever? God's word and people's souls.

My Heart's Cry to You, O Lord

Father, thank you for allowing me the joy and privilege of a busy and fulfilling career. But may I offer an even greater "thank you?" I'm so grateful that you tugged at my heartstrings to invest in the community around me outside of work. I've never been so content and fulfilled as I am today. My heart is full because I'm finally able to connect more deeply, fellowship consistently, and serve to my heart's desire. Thank you for showing me the path home and helping me to never take for granted the brief time we are here on earth to know Christ and make him known. Amen.

Practicing Grace & Gratitude

1. ***Grace & gratitude from God.*** "You, my brothers and sisters, were called to be free." Each evening this week, I'll reflect on my day and prayerfully revisit how I spent my time, remembering that I have limited hours and days in this life. I want to rightly prioritize my time by investing in that which lasts for eternity.
2. ***Grace & gratitude in me.*** "But do not use your freedom to indulge the flesh; rather, serve one another humbly in love." This week, I'll review my calendar and study where I invest my time. I'll take special note of how I spend my off-duty and leisure hours. If I need to adjust because I see imbalance or misplaced priorities, I'll put corrective measures in place.
3. ***Grace & gratitude in life.*** "For the entire law is fulfilled in keeping this one command: 'Love your neighbor as yourself.'" One question I'll ask myself this week is this: "Do I love others as I love myself?" Do I sacrifice my time, my energy, and my material goods for the benefit and welfare of those around me? If I don't, then I'll begin incorporating one small change each week.

Chapter 29

Grace-Filled Gratitude Changes How We Interpret the World

Finally, be strong in the Lord and in his mighty power. Put on the full armor of God, so that you can take your stand against the devil's schemes. For our struggle is not against flesh and blood, but against the rulers, against the authorities, against the powers of this dark world and against the spiritual forces of evil in the heavenly realms.

Ephesians 6:10–12

As we look at the condition of the world today, so utterly hostile to the gospel, we must also look at the sovereignty of God and at His promises. He has promised to redeem people from every nation, and He has commanded us to make disciples of all nations. We must, then, trust God by praying. We must learn to trust God, not only in the adverse circumstances of our individual lives, but also in the adverse circumstances of the Church as a whole.

Jerry Bridges

Cathy, Lori, and Renee were committed to staying as healthy as possible, so they made a pact to walk three miles every weekday afternoon. As friends and sisters in the Lord, this trio shared much more than an hour together exercising their bodies. On most days as they walked, they took turns talking about their individual spiritual journey with the Lord and what he was teaching them. Back and forth, the uplifting and often hilarious banter would go as they huffed and puffed their way through their neighborhood. Each of these women agreed that between the walking and the talking, they could take on the world together.

Until recently, that is. On one chilly afternoon right before Thanksgiving during their walk, they all took turns sighing at various intervals. Finally, they stopped and looked at each other with raised eyebrows.

Cathy was the first to admit that she was fighting feelings of constant anxiety. "I just can't seem to stay away from the news," she said. "And then I'm all upset for the rest of the day." she said in discouragement.

Lori commiserated before adding her own confession of feeling angry when she scrolled through the news on her phone each morning. "Everything just seems wrong!"

Lastly, Renee chimed in, sharing how frustrated she became whenever she turned on the radio in the car to listen to her favorite programs. "I feel irritated when I hear about so much trouble and unrest throughout the world."

They all sighed again and then resumed their walk. After a while, they simultaneously experienced an "aha" moment. "What's the common denominator here, ladies?" Lori asked. "The news! Whether it's checking for stories first thing in the morning on our phones, driving in our cars listening to the radio, or watching the nightly news—it's all too much to take in, process, and then let go."

"Let's make another pact," Cathy suggested. "From this day forward, we commit to staying away from our phones, the radio, and the television each day until we have first spent time with the Lord reading our Bibles and praying. How can we expect to think like the overcomers Jesus says we are if we don't prioritize him before we expose ourselves to everything that's wrong in the world?"

"Makes sense to me," Renee agreed.

As Cathy, Lori, and Renee each worked to uphold the pact they made, they quickly realized how right Lori was when she pointed out the wisdom of "no news before the good news."

When we allow the world and its troubles to infiltrate our hearts and minds before we spend time with God, we're ill-equipped to handle the magnitude of sorrow we see, read, or hear. Only when we place things in their proper order—God first and then everything else—can we expect to view the world's brokenness through the lens of hope and eternity.

Certainly, we can't live with our heads in the sand and ignore the worldwide happenings, but we have to put first things first. That first thing is time spent daily with our heavenly Father so that he can renew our minds. In days like these, when unrest is the norm, each of us needs the timeless truths of God's word to penetrate our hearts and minds day by day, hour by hour. As Cathy, Lori, and Renee found out after they put their "no news before the good news" policy into play, their attitudes changed. Their emotions lifted. Their walk and talk became energized, and they became more fit to serve God with an attitude of grace-infused trust and a heart full of gratitude for the Lord's constant presence and provision.

No matter what's happening in your home, your town, your state, your country, or the world, God still sovereignly rules. This powerful biblical truth should give us inner peace, robust hope, and the spirit of an overcomer. God is on the throne. Jesus lives to intercede for us. The Holy Spirit dwells within us. That is the good news we need to focus on!

Take-away Action Thought

When my emotions begin to spiral because I feel overwhelmed by the news of the day, I'll turn off my phone, turn off the radio, and turn off the television. Then I'll turn my attention to reading my Bible and praying. I will remind myself of the good news of Jesus Christ and that God is ruler over all the nations.

My Heart's Cry to You, O Lord

Father, today I was utterly overwhelmed by suffering and pain from all parts of the world. I felt helpless to make a difference. And then I began to feel depressed and anxious because I can't control any of the unrest that seems to escalate every day. Help me to keep my heart and mind focused on you. Give me the wisdom to realize that you are fully in control and that you see what is happening. Lord, I need your grace and strength to not fear what I witness taking place in our world today. I need your abiding presence and power to overcome my worries, fears, and doubts. Amen.

Practicing Grace & Gratitude

1. ***Grace & gratitude from God.*** "Finally be strong in the Lord and in his mighty power." Each day this week, I'll prioritize time spent reading the Bible and praying before I engage with the news. I want my focus to be on God's sovereignty and on seeing this broken world through the lens of hope and eternity.
2. ***Grace & gratitude in me.*** "Put on the full armor of God, so that you can take your stand against the devil's schemes." Each morning, I'll figuratively put on the full armor of God by reading Ephesians 6 and reciting it out loud.
3. ***Grace & gratitude in life.*** "For our struggle is not against flesh and blood, but against the rulers, against the authorities, against the powers of this dark world and against the spiritual forces of evil in the heavenly realms." Each evening this week, I'll spend time writing out specific prayer requests, being mindful that my struggle in this life isn't really with other people, adverse situations, or personal disappointments. My struggle is against spiritual forces that oppose God and his children.

Chapter 30

Grace-Filled Gratitude Changes How We Worship God

I lift up my eyes to the mountains—
where does my help come from?
My help comes from the LORD,
the Maker of heaven and earth.
He will not let your foot slip—
he who watches over you will not slumber;
indeed, he who watches over Israel
will neither slumber or sleep.
The LORD watches over you—
the LORD is your shade at your right hand;
the sun will not harm you by day,
nor the moon by night.
The LORD will keep you from all harm—
he will watch over your life;
the LORD will watch over your coming and going
both now and forevermore.

Psalm 121

I used to think that God's gifts were on shelves—one above another—and the taller we grow, the easier we can reach them. Now I find that God's gifts are on shelves—and the lower we stoop, the more we get.

F. B. Meyer

I sat alongside many other dear folks from my church fellowship as we listened intently to the close family members of a recently deceased gentleman share stories from his long and fruitful life. As this beloved Christian man's youngest sister stood to talk, she regaled us with both comical and poignant tales about her well-loved oldest brother. One story followed another until I was able to form a clear picture of this man's life as a boy growing up in a Christian home.

From early on, their father would read Psalm 121 before each family trip or vacation. He would sit his family down at the table and read the entire psalm before they left. That simple habit of committing their traveling to the Lord before they stepped out the door became a lifelong tradition for the entire family and was passed down to the next generation.

As we listened to this beautiful reminiscence, it was apparent that everyone felt the deeper meaning of this simple habit, which was later passed down from generation to generation. Clearly, as they listened to the lyrical words of Psalm 121, this family quietly worshiped God and thanked him for his present and perfect provision no matter where their feet went. Each one of them thanked him for his grace and goodness as they traveled through life. Truly, as they humbly committed their next steps to him, they worshiped. As they gave thanks, they worshiped.

Our mutual friend's passing into the presence of Jesus was necessarily bittersweet. Yes, he will most assuredly be missed. And yes, we all rejoice because we know he is with our Lord and Savior Jesus Christ. Absent from the body. Present with the

Lord. What a legacy of faith, hope, and love he left for those who follow behind him. May we all travel as this man of faith did.

As we journey through life and experience its ups and downs, we can emulate this dear family's example by committing our way to Jesus with every step we take. The more we immerse ourselves in Scripture and allow its powerful truths to penetrate our hearts and minds, the more we become worshipers of the Most High.

No matter where our feet step, we can be confident of God's abiding presence, guidance, and protection. As this psalm reminds us, "My help comes from the LORD, the Maker of heaven and earth." What better way is there to begin and end our journey through this life than by humbling ourselves and acknowledging God's sovereignty and careful rule over all of life?

As we become dedicated students through careful study of his word and obedience to his commands, we learn how to be better worshipers. As we walk with Jesus and keep in step with the Spirit, we learn God's ways and continually discover that God's glory and goodness cover us from all harm. Sure, we will always face challenges, hardships, and grievous circumstances in this sin-ridden world. But through all of it, we can be eternally secure in the faithful grip of our Lord. Come what may, we can give thanks for an amazing eternal truth:

> The LORD will keep you from all harm—he will watch over your life; the LORD will watch over your coming and going both now and forevermore.

Take-away Action Thought

When I arise in the morning, I will give thanks for God's sovereign protection and presence in my life. During the day, I will give thanks for his careful administration, so evident in my daily life. In the evening, I will worship God and give thanks for his watching over my coming and going, both now and forevermore.

My Heart's Cry to You, O Lord

Father, this life is a journey that sometimes takes me places I'd rather not go. I often feel as though I'm not up to the challenges before me. My steps falter, my strength wanes, and even my faith seems inadequate for the tasks before me. Please help me to remember to start off my day right by talking to you first thing in the morning and continue conversing with you throughout the day. Help me to remember your endless faithfulness toward me. Remind me of your present loving care. And bolster my spirit to face tomorrow fully confident in your promised supply of grace and strength. I worship you. I thank you. I love you. Amen.

Practicing Grace & Gratitude

1. *Grace & gratitude from God.* "The LORD will keep you from all harm—he will watch over your life; the Lord will watch over your coming and going both now and forevermore." In my journal, I'll reflect on God's protection and provision for me this week. I'll make sure to

write down all the pertinent details so that in the coming days and months, when I'm tempted to doubt in God's perfect provision, these accounts will remind me of his faithful love and care for me.

2. ***Grace & gratitude in me.*** "I lift up my eyes to the mountains—where does my help come from? My help comes from the LORD, the Maker of heaven and earth." Each morning this week, I'll spend time thanking the Lord in advance for all the promised help he will give me as needs arise. I'll write this verse down and carry it with me to remind me of his promise to help me no matter what, no matter when, and no matter how.

3. ***Grace & gratitude in life.*** "He will not let your foot slip—he who watches over you will not slumber; indeed, he who watches over Israel will neither slumber or sleep. The LORD watches over you—the LORD is your shade at your right hand; the sun will not harm you by day, nor the moon by night." This week, I'll be on the lookout for others who need encouragement. I will gently remind them of his faithfulness and loving care toward them and then look for ways to be Jesus' hands and feet of service toward them. In all that I say or do, I want my life to be an act of worship to God.

Sources for Quotations

1. Randy Alcorn, *90 Days of God's Goodness* (Colorado Springs: Multnomah, 2011), 219–20.
2. Edward Welch, *A Small Book for the Anxious Heart* (Greensboro: New Growth Press, 2019), 99.
3. Jerry Bridges, *Trusting God* (Colorado Springs: NavPress, 1988), 52.
4. Elisabeth Elliot, *Suffering Is Never for Nothing* (Nashville: B&H, 2011), 77.
5. Nancy Leigh DeMoss, *Choosing Gratitude* (Chicago: Moody, 2009), 139.
6. Elliot, *Suffering Is Never for Nothing*, 75.
7. Welch, *A Small Book for the Anxious Heart*, 113.
8. Welch, *A Small Book for the Anxious Heart*, 146.
9. DeMoss, *Choosing Gratitude*, 112.
10. Paul David Tripp, *New Morning Mercies* (Wheaton, IL: Crossway, 2014), March 2 entry.
11. Tripp, *New Morning Mercies*, October 14 entry.
12. Tripp, *New Morning Mercies*, September 23 entry.
13. Alcorn, *90 Days of God's Goodness*, 111.
14. Nancy Leigh DeMoss, *Choosing Forgiveness* (Chicago: Moody, 2008), 76.
15. Paul David Tripp, *War of Words* (Phillipsburg, NJ: P&R, 2000), 110.

16. DeMoss, *Choosing Gratitude*, 144.
17. Charles Spurgeon, *The Power of Prayer in a Believer's Life* (Lynwood: Emerald Books, 2016), 174.
18. Saint Augustine, *Confessions*, trans. Henry Chadwick, Oxford World's Classics (Oxford: Oxford University Press, 1991), 96.
19. John MacArthur, *Anxious for Nothing: God's Cure for the Cares of Your Soul*, 3rd ed. (Colorado Springs: David C. Cook, 2012).
20. Elyse Fitzpatrick, *Because He Loves Me* (Wheaton, IL: Crossway, 2008), 118.
21. Welch, *A Small Book for the Anxious Heart*, 173.
22. Kathy Carlton Willis, *Wit, Whimsy & Wisdom* (Beaumont: 3G Books, 2021), 31–32.
23. William Tyndale, quoted in Ralph S. Werrell, *The Blood of Christ in the Theology of William Tyndale* (Cambridge: James Clarke & Co., 2015), 158.
24. A.W. Tozer (online quote).
25. Paul David Tripp, *Instruments in the Redeemer's Hands* (Phillipsburg, NJ: P&R, 2002), 106–7.
26. Randy Alcorn, *Happiness* (Carol Stream: Tyndale House, 2015), 428.
27. Paula Rinehart, *Better Than My Dreams* (Nashville: Nelson, 2007), 95–96.
28. Jonathan Edwards, *Representative Selections* (New York: Hill and Wang, 1962), 38.
29. Bridges, *Trusting God*, 91–92.
30. F. B. Meyer, quoted in Ann Voskamp, *One Thousand Gifts: A Dare to Live Fully Right Where You Are* (Grand Rapids: Zondervan, 201).

Books by Michele Howe from Hendrickson Publishing Group

Big Feelings, Bigger God

Burdens Do a Body Good: Meeting Life's Challenges with Strength (and Soul) (with Dr. Christopher A. Foetisch)

Caring for Your Aging Parents: Lessons in Love, Loss, and Letting Go

Deliver Us: Finding Hope in the Psalms for Moments of Desperation

Empty Nest, What's Next? Parenting Adult Children Without Losing Your Mind

Finding Freedom and Joy in Self-Forgetfulness

Giving Thanks for a Perfectly Imperfect Life

Going It Alone: Meeting the Challenges of Being a Single Mom

Joyous Faith: The Key to Aging with Resilience

Living Bravely: Super Incredible Faith Devotional (for kids ages 6–9)

Navigating the Friendship Maze: The Search for Authentic Friendship

Preparing, Adjusting, and Loving the Empty Nest A companion to *Empty Nest, What's Next?*

Still Going It Alone: Mothering with Faith and Finesse When the Children Have Grown

Strength for All Seasons: A Prayer Devotional

There's a Reason They Call It GRANDparenting

Visual Bible Verse Devotions